Origins
of the
American Short Story

Origins

of the

American Short Story

Edited by Wolfgang Hochbruck,
Aynur Erdogan, Philipp Fidler

Slack Water Press
Los Gatos, California

Slack Water Press, Los Gatos 95032

Copyright © 2008 Wolfgang Hochbruck
All rights reserved.

ISBN 978-0-9797613-1-7

Library of Congress Control Number: 2008928013

Cover design by Theis und Partner

Cover image: Boston Harbor, from the *Royal American Magazine,* January 1774 (Paul Revere, engraving)

The paper used in this publication is acid free and meets all ANSI standards for archival quality paper.

c. pf

Contents

Preface
vii

Introduction
Wolfgang Hochbruck
3

Adventure of a Young English Officer
Among the Abenakee Savages
Anonymous
13

The Desperate Negroe
Anonymous (Rev. James Ramsay)
29

Yonora: An American Indian Tale
Melpomene
45

Account of a Swiss Captain
Anonymous
63

Story of Julia: A Real Character
Punctilio
73

Fidele: Or the Faithful Shepherd
Caloc
101

The Story of the Captain's Wife and an Aged Woman
Ruri Colla
121

Something Unaccountable
Z. P.
139

Narrative of the Unpardonable Sin
N.
153

The Adventure of the German Student
Washington Irving
169

Magazine Sources
185

Further Reading
187

Preface

The present collection differs from traditional anthologies of American short stories in two ways: first, we added an extensive commentary to each story to provide a detailed background, a publication history, and notes to facilitate reading and understanding texts that were first printed almost two and a half centuries ago. Second, we broadened the focus for our selections from American topics and other typically American features to an investigation into the origins and the nature of the short story genre. Our main goal is to show how the short story began to emerge as a result of the American magazine culture in the late 18th century, and in particular, how various types of short texts, such as, tale, sketch, historiette, and anecdote, contributed to its emergence.

In his 1963 doctoral dissertation, Jack B. Moore identified some 400 early American magazine texts as "short stories." Moore's approach in making this selection was predominantly thematic, focusing on American topics and characters. We widened his focus to include features that have become part of the modern short story, such as calculated brevity and textual ambiguity. However, our collection remains within the range of texts that Moore identified and that he claimed are the best examples of the emerging short story genre. One result is that the range and the number of stories selected for this volume are representative rather than exhaustive. However, all of them are presented here for the first time in a critical edition with notes and commentary.

Much of the research that went into this edition was originally undertaken by research assistants who prepared drafts of the notes and commentaries for the present edition. While these contributions required considerable additional editorial work, we retained the names of the assistants at the end of each commentary in recognition of their effort.

The editors are grateful to Jon Adams at Slack Water Press for his unfaltering support for an unusual project, and we hope that this volume will serve as an example for future projects.

WH, AE, PF
Freiburg, June 2008

Origins
of the
American Short Story

Introduction

Wolfgang Hochbruck

None of the texts in this volume were originally called short stories. As has been often repeated, the term *short-story*, then still with a hyphen, was made popular by Brander Matthews; its common usage is decidedly a 20th century phenomenon. However, literary historians and critics all agree that the 19th century already saw the rise of the short story *avant la lettre*, but there is still considerable disagreement as to where and when the first early or proto-short stories became available. Among the scholars working in the field, Jack B. Moore, Edward W. R. Pitcher, and Eugene Current-Garcia stand out. More recently, James Nagel has edited the first comprehensive anthology of short stories, including an entire section covering the period before 1820.[1] The late 18th century proto-short stories coalesce from different directions, with the various texts coming under headings like tale, (true) story, (character) sketch, anecdote, historiette, essay, and fragment. The very range of terms used for the types of texts points to the diversity of influences on the emerging form of the short story.

The relationship between these forms needs to be further explored, even though the general problem—that there are never any absolutely clear lines of demarcation—will in all likelihood continue to thwart efforts in this direction.[2] A further complication lies in the fact that the canon of subgenres is, and has always been, incomplete. It should be noted that, while there is the *essay* and the *sketch*—neither of which are first and foremost literary terms—there is no such thing in British or American letters as a *study,* in contrast to *etude* in music, and *Studie* in German, both accessible terms in the late 18th and early 19th centuries. Several of the texts in this volume appear to be related to the *study,* and they are similar to some of Poe's tale-like studies that are part of the emerging short story.

One conclusion that may be drawn from this fact is that subgenre categories in and of themselves cannot be expected to answer the question of the generic origins of the short story. A genre theory of the short story would therefore in all likelihood fare better if it were descriptive.[3] However, Fred Lewis Pattee's 1923 declaration that "Rip van Winkle" and "The Legend of Sleepy Hollow" are the first American short stories not only set a norm, but also cut off the genre discussion, stating that the impact and influence of any and all forerunners of the short story were "negligible."[4] In the decade preceding Pattee, scholars had already ventured closer to a descriptive theory. For example, Clayton Hamilton called the principle of the short story its "economy of means."[5]

Before 1800, however, this "economy of means" usually spelled *relative* rather than *calculated* brevity, to use Barbara Korte's term, in which the space taken by the text was determined by the lines the magazine editor allotted, rather than by the author's conscious use of innovative textual features.[6] And no matter what the formal specifics, the central feature of most of the early short prose that appeared in magazines is their unquestioned "subjugation of fiction to an unwritten code of socio-moral utilitarianism."[7] This was clearly detrimental to the formal development of the new genre, since as with all other forms of predominantly ideological texts, moral purpose and didacticism do not result in an appealing formal structure. This is one of the reasons why most literary texts written for a clearly defined audience and imbued with a moral, political, or other purposeful message are, at best, of mediocre aesthetic quality.

The early short story moved away from the simplicity of didacticism and moral purpose by moving toward the complexity of textual form. As Pitcher points out, the beginning of short fiction in America is found

> in the gradual coming together of forms such as anecdote, fable, tall tale and sentimental story with the increasingly diverse aspirations, images, character types, and historic incidents of a people linked by language and culture to Britain and Europe.[8]

What constituted this "coming together"? Rather than attempting to delineate how much of the essay or the sketch went into each story (see the *Critical Commentary* on the individual stories in this volume), I will attempt to outline a brief hypothesis of how the American short story may have emerged.

The early short story is constructed at a crossroads of several short prose and fiction sub-genres that make use of a variety of textual features. From the tale, it retains the narrative plot structure, with variants that borrow the moral point format of the anecdote, and the descriptive format of the sketch. This latter variant often appears in the late 18th century magazine under its own heading as *fragment*. From the pamphlet and the sermon, the early short stories derive a rhetorical sense of direction and purpose. From the essay, finally, comes a highly important feature: that of a rationalizing and argumentative structure, which projects the short story form away from the mono-directional meaning that usually governs the moralizing and didactic tale of the 18th century, and thus opens up the text for literary ambiguities. This is the main paradigm shift from the proto-short story forms to the early short story texts, a shift that moves the short story away from a moral purpose and toward a unity of effect.

Unity of effect, in turn, has often been misunderstood as a pointed plot, and treated as such by Brander Matthews and the O. Henry school of short story writing. The original meaning of unity of effect in Poe's review, "Nathaniel Hawthorne: Twice-Told Tales," was more likely an aspect of the aesthetics of reception. Note that Poe continues his discussion of the tale as follows: "And by such means, with care and skill, a picture is at length painted which leaves in the mind of him who contemplates it with a kindred art, a sense of the fullest satisfaction."[9] The effect may of course be achieved by hearing a sermon, or reading a pamphlet, that makes use of its rhetorical means in such a way as to be satisfyingly convincing. It is also apparent how a similar effect may be attained by the argumentative, rationalizing structure of the essay, weighing arguments and drawing the reader into a complicity of wit. Applied to the tale, the essayistic mode of argumentation, however, will result in a greater ambiguity of purpose, and create an additional reading interest precisely because there is no longer just one predetermined meaning.

It was this convergence and transformation, and the ensuing paradigm shift from moral purpose to unity of effect, that created the early short story between the

Declaration of Independence and Washington Irving's *Sketch Book*. When focusing on periodical magazines, the scope can be narrowed even further to the decades around the turn of the 18th to the 19th century. At the same time, the Postal Act of 1794 did more than many textual developments to foster magazine reading and publishing. By providing special mailing rates for magazines, it enabled more magazines to be started from 1794 to 1800 than in the fifty years before. According to Frank L. Mott, the Postal Act of 1794 also marks the dividing line between the *Period of the Beginnings* and the *Period of Nationalism*, which in turn ended with Andrew Jackson's first presidency in 1825.[10] The first signs of the rise of the American short story as a textual genre, however, can be traced to the years just before the War of Independence.

Three basic criteria were used for including texts in the present collection of American short stories. The first is the evident use of American topicality, themes, settings, and characters, which Jack B. Moore already used as a measuring rod. The second is that they go beyond the merely didactically functional; that is, there must be a degree of artistic form recognizable in the shape of the narrative, or at least the form must be so openly structured that a certain variety of readings and meanings is possible. And the third is the reader reception: At least two of the stories collected in this volume show how potentially ambiguous readings and varieties of meaning enter the text through a change in the publication context. "The Adventure of a Young English Officer Among the Abenakee Savages" takes on its ambiguity from the political situation of its republication at the beginning of the American Revolution. A similar case is exemplified by "The Desperate Negroe." In contrast, the "Narrative of the

Unpardonable Sin," because of its contextual place of publication in a religious journal, was in all likelihood intended to convey a single, Christian meaning directed at the sin of blasphemy; it derives its ambiguity from the open construction of potential meanings in the text itself, as does "Something Unaccountable." These and the other texts in the collection all show a degree of artistic skill and ingenuity, as well as American or at least Americanized meaning, and textual features that were to become central to the modern short story.

These stories show an increasing awareness of their own form, and they show a calculated brevity and an effect that gradually replaces the kind of textual uncertainty that appears, for example, in "Yonora," which breaks off unpremeditatedly right after introducing a new storyline. The arrangement of the stories in the collection mirrors both chronological and thematic shifts. The first group is made up of visibly "colonial" texts; the second group of modified moral or didactic tales; and the third group of proto-modern ambiguities and uncertainties of meaning.

With texts like Washington Irving's "The Adventure of the German Student," which closes this volume, the nascent early short story gives way to the fully developed specimen, and to literary masters like Poe, Hawthorne, and Melville. Irving himself recognized this development in a letter to Henry Brevoort, commenting that "in these shorter writings, every page must have its merit. The author must be continually piquant; woe to him if he makes an awkward sentence or writes a stupid page; the critics are sure to pounce upon it."[11]

The increasing focus on form shows how the shift from the moral focus of the 18th century essay to the entertainment focus of literature results in a variety of possible interpretations that were accessible to the learned and well-read middle-class reader. It was this part of the hegemonic block of readers that the new short story was aimed at; it was this group that responded most positively to the new genre; and it was this group that bought the stories when they later came out, like Irving's, in book form.

It is also only logical that around the same time the authors gradually gave up the inherited British mode of anonymity. Most of the stories collected in this volume that are likely to be of American origin are already signed, if only with *noms de plume* or initials. The strategy of initializing or using encoded names gradually gives way, around this time, to public uncovering of the real identities, as in the cases of Sarah Wentworth Morton and Judith Sargent Murray. Joseph Dennie, as editor of the first predominantly *literary* magazine, the *Port Folio* (1801–1827), was the first to give up the pose of anonymity altogether. Within another decade, the encoded names were a thing of the past, and the short story an established new type of fiction. The first comprehensive poetological discourse on the principles of composition guiding the author of this kind of new fiction, aiming to achieve what Irving yet called "piquancy," is of course Poe in his "The Philosophy of Composition," as well as in the review "Nathaniel Hawthorne: Twice-Told Tales." Significantly, both texts originally appeared in a magazine: *Graham's*, in 1842 and 1846. Klaus Lubbers has summarized Poe's poetology in the "Philosophy," pointing out its four main aspects. First, the dependence of the composition on its limited length is determined, in turn, by the intended unity of effect. Theme and tone, though second to effect and extent take precedence over setting and actual plot.

Second, writing is a combinatory process, a calculated construction of a network of meaning. Third, the sobriety of calculation and the conscious spirit of composition deny romantic concepts such as "fine frenzy" and "ecstatic intuition" as driving forces. Finally, the qualities ultimately deciding the artistic value of a text are complexity and suggestiveness.[12]

Looking back at the emergence of the short story, the extent to which it entailed a major overhaul of textual form becomes visible. Before the 1780s, lack of form was one of the characteristics of the short prose narrative. Imposing structure and order meant a transformation of this formlessness into form; containing the text within a range of relative brevity meant economizing the text; the fusion of methods and techniques from several different genres meant their convergence. In this combination, the short story as a genre was also prototypically the most visible literary form and expression of early American literature.

Notes

[1] Jack B. Moore, *Native Elements in American Short Fiction: 1741–1800* (Chapel Hill: U of North Carolina, 1963); Edward W. R. Pitcher, ed., *An Anthology of the Short Story in 18th and 19th Century America*, 2 vols. (Lewiston: Edwin Mellen P, 2000); Eugene Current-Garcia, *The American Short Story before 1850: A Critical History* (Boston: Twayne, 1985); James Nagel, *Anthology of the American Short Story* (Boston: Houghton Mifflin, 2007). His selection includes two stories also reprinted here, "The Adventure of an English Officer Among the Abenakee

Savages" and "The Story of the Captain's Wife and an Aged Woman."

[2] Franz Link, who attempts to distinguish between at least some of the categories, manages to define the essay and the sketch apart from the short story, but the category of the tale remains hazy. "'Tale,' 'Sketch' 'Essay' und 'Short Story'," *Die amerikanische Kurzgeschichte: Theorie und Entwicklung*, ed., Hans Bungert (Darmstadt: WBG, 1972): 211–21.

[3] See for instance Paul Goetsch's descriptive approach, which establishes the way most short stories arrive at—or retain—their relative brevity as a result of consciously applying textual techniques. "Die Begrenzung der Short Story," *Die amerikanische Short Story*, ed. Hans Bungert (Darmstadt: WBG, 1972): 368–87.

[4] Fred L. Pattee, *The Development of the Short Story in America: An Historical Survey* (New York: Harper, 1923): 1.

[5] Clayton Hamilton, *Materials of Fiction* (New York: Doubleday, Page, 1912): 175.

[6] Barbara Korte, *The Short Story in Britain* (Tübingen: Francke UTB, 2003): 5.

[7] Edward W. R. Pitcher, "Introduction," *An Anthology of the Short Story in 18th and 19th Century America*, 1: 3.

[8] Pitcher, "Introduction," 1: 1.

[9] Edgar A. Poe, "Nathaniel Hawthorne: Twice-Told Tales," *The Complete Works of Edgar Allan Poe*, ed. James A. Harrison, 17 vols. (New York: AMS P, 1965) 11: 108.

[10] Frank Luther Mott, *A History of American Magazines: 1741–1850* (Cambridge, MA: Harvard UP, 1957): 94, 340.

[11] Washington Irving, *The Life and Letters of Washington Irving*, ed. Pierre M. Irving, 3 vols. (New York: Putnam's Sons, 1869) 2: 5.

[12] Klaus Lubbers, *Typologie der Short Story* (Darmstadt: WBG, 1989): 3.

Adventure of a Young English Officer
Among the Abenakee Savages
Anonymous

Reprinted, translated, and rewritten at least thirty times over a span of about thirty years in various magazines and books in the United States, Britain, France, and even Germany, the "Adventure of a Young English Officer Among the Abenakee Savages" ranks as one of the most popular stories of 18th century magazine culture.[1] It has also been included in modern anthologies, but its actual origins in France eluded both editors and critics. The second American printing appeared in the February issue of the Royal American Magazine *in 1775; this is the form in which it is reprinted here.*

Isaiah Thomas published the first issue of the Royal American Magazine or Universal Repository of Instruction and Amusement *in January 1774. The title was somewhat ironic; in his own words Thomas was a "bold patriot-printer," and the magazine a mouthpiece of the American colonists. The* Royal American Magazine *lasted only fourteen months; Thomas himself resigning in June 1774 because of "the Distresses of the Town of Boston, by the shutting up of our Port, and throwing all Ranks of Men into Confusion." He proposed to suspend publication until "the Affairs of this Country are a little better settled."[2] The following month's issue was published by Joseph Greenleaf.*

At the end of the year, Greenleaf in turn confronted his readers with some of the problems he had encountered during his months as editor. He apologized for the bad quality of ink and paper, but claimed that since the ink "was of American manufacture [his] customers were not only willing but desirous that [he] should use it."[3] Three months later the magazine was discontinued.

Since "Adventure of a Young English Officer Among the Abenakee Savages" was originally published in French, it may at first seem quixotic to claim that it is an American story. However, the argument for its Americanness is not based on the genesis of the story but on the social and political circumstances of its American publication. Where earlier readers identified with the English officer in the story, American readers, especially those on the road to open warfare with England in 1775, were more likely to identify with the Native American.

Adventure of a Young English Officer Among the Abenakee Savages

During the last war in America, a band of Savages having surprised and defeated a party of the English, such of those as were not actually killed on the spot had very little chance of getting away from enemies who were much more quick of foot than they, and who, pursuing them with unrelenting fury, used those whom they overtook with a barbarity almost without example, even in those countries.[4]

A young English officer, pressed by two Savages who were making at him with uplifted hatchets, had not the least hope of escaping death, and tho't[5] of nothing now but to sell his life as dear as he could. Just then, an old Savage, armed with a bow, drew near him, in an act to pierce him with an arrow; but after taking aim at him, all of a sudden he drops his point, and runs to throw himself between the young Englishman and the two Barbarians, who were going to massacre him. These drew back out of respect to the motions of the old man, who, with signs of peace, took the officer by the hand, after removing his apprehensions by friendly gestures, and carried him home with him to his hut. There he treated him with great humanity and gentleness, less like his slave than his companion. He taught him the Abenakee language, and the coarse arts in use among those people. They lived very well satisfied with each other. One only point of the old man's deportment could not but give the young officer some uneasiness; he would some times surprize the savage fixing his eyes upon him, when, after looking long and steadfastly at him, he would let fall some tears.

However, on the return of the spring the Abenakees took the field again, and proceeded in quest of the English.

The old man, who had still remains of vigour enough to bear the fatigues of war, went along with his countrymen, not forgetting to take his prisoner with him. They made a march of about two hundred leagues, through the trackless wilds and forests of that country, till at length they came within view of a plain, in which they discovered an English camp.[6] This the old Savage shewed to his companion, at the same time eyeing him wishfully, and marking his countenance, "There (says he) are thy brothers waiting to give us battle. What sayest thou? I preserved thee from death. I have taught thee to build canoes; to make bows and arrows; to catch the deer of the forest; to wield the hatchet; with all our arts of war. What wast thou when I took thee home to my dwelling? Thy hands were as the hands of a mere child, they could serve thee but little for thy defence, and less yet for providing thee means of sustenance. Thy soul was in the dark; thou wert a stranger to all necessary knowledge. To me thou owest life, the means of life, every thing—Couldest thou then be ungrateful enough to go over to join thy countrymen, and to lift the hatchet against us?"

The young Englishman made answer that he should, it was true, have a just repugnance to carrying arms against those of his own nation, but that he would never turn them against the Abenakees, whom, so long as he should live, he would consider as his brothers.

At this the Savage dejected his head and lifting up his hands he covered his face with them, as it were in a deep meditation. After he had remained some time in this attitude, he looked earnestly at the English officer and said to him in a tone of grief, mixed with tenderness, "Hast thou a father?"—"He was alive," answered the young man, "when I left my country." "Oh, how unhappy must he be!" said the Savage—After a moment's pause he added, "Dost thou not know that I too was once a father? Alas! I am no longer one. No; I am no longer a father! I saw my son fall in battle. He fought by the side of me, I saw him die like a man, die, covered with wounds as he fell. But I revenged him."

As he pronounced these words with the most pathetic emphasis, he shuddered; he seemed to breathe with pain, choked with inward groans, which he was endeavouring to stifle. His eyes looked wild, but no tears came from them. Little by little the violence of his agitations ceased: He grew calm, and turning towards the east, he pointed to the rising sun, and said to the young Englishman, "Seest thou yon beauteous luminary, the sun in all its splendour? Does the sight of it afford thee any pleasure?" "Undoubtedly," answered the officer, "who can behold so fine a sky without delight?"—"And yet to me it no longer gives any!" says the Savage. After pronouncing these few words he turned, and casting his eye on a bush in full flower, "See!" said he, "young man, does not that gay appearance of flowers give thee a sort of joy to look at it?" "It does, indeed," replied the officer. "And yet," says the old man, "it delights not me!" adding, with some degree of impetuosity, "Depart—haste—fly to yon camp of thy friends. Get home, that thy father may still see, with pleasure, the rising of the sun, and the flowers of the spring."

Critical Commentary

Of the stories in this collection, the "Adventure of a Young English Officer Among the Abenakee Savages" has had the most colorful publication history. As far as can be ascertained, there were at least nineteen editions. This publication history is reiterated here in some detail to show that the early short story was a transnational genre, in the sense that largely the same sentiments were transported within the reading classes in the 18th century. However, with the American printing, these common sentiments no longer applied because, in the confrontation between the Indian and the officer, American readers probably identified with the American Indian rather than the English officer, or, if they were loyalists, they may have wondered which side they were on.

The first version of the story that has surfaced so far was printed in the French *Gazette littéraire de l'Europe* in February 1765.[7] The author may have been Jean-François de Saint-Lambert in whose *Contes Americains* it was reprinted in 1769, titled "L'Abenaki."[8] By then, however, the story had taken on a life of its own: a mere three weeks after the first printing, an English translation appeared in the *Gentleman's Magazine*. This is all the more noteworthy for the fact that merely two years had passed since the end of the Seven Years' War, in which Abenakis had fought alongside their French allies.[9] To depict them as humane and feeling lay in the interest of a British public into whose ownership Canada had changed hands in 1763.

The version that appeared in December 1765 in the German *Hamburgisches Journal* was probably adapted and translated from the French original. It reduced the story's structure to those parts interesting to a German public without political involvement in the North American situation, and consequently focused on the arts of war, and on the sentimental aspect. This version includes, for example, the art of scalping which is mentioned in the French version but not in any of the English versions found so far.[10]

Possibly in reaction to this curtailed version, a second German translation saw print in the *Hannoverisches Journal*. This translation is more precise both in its choice of words and its reconstruction of the plot. It also mentions the *Gentleman's Magazine* as source.[11]

The first American version of the story appeared in 1767 in *Bickerstaff's Boston Almanack* edited by Benjamin West, who used the pen name of Isaac Bickerstaff, a character originally invented by Jonathan Swift. This is a typical pirated reprint, without reference to authorship or source but identical to the version in the *Gentleman's Magazine*, except for an added illustration which enhances the drama of the situation. The English officer armed, curiously enough, with a lance is shown opposite the old man and the two hatchet-wielding warriors. The caption of the woodcut reads "A sachem of the Abenakee Nation, rescuing an English Officer from the Indians." The background is idealized with two rows of trees vaguely reminiscent of an English park.[12]

After this reprint, the topic seems to have been exhausted for a while. When the text appeared next, after a seven year gap, in the version reprinted here from the February issue of the *Royal American Magazine*, the political situation had changed, resulting in a rearticulation of meanings.[13] This 1775 "Among the Abenakee Savages" presents an important step in the development toward the short story, both on the formal as well as on the content level. As a narrative text, it shows qualities lifting it above the average for the period: Mixing dialogue and narrative passages, it creates two plausible figures and a credible emotional situation, and it especially succeeds in gradually building up a tension of increasing anticipation. Given the stereotyping of Native Americans, notably those allied with the French, the reader is invited to wonder what might have caused the sudden change in the old Abenaki's behavior when he "throws himself between the young Englishman and the two Barbarians, who were going to massacre him." The second moment pointing in the same direction is when the old man actually sheds tears "after looking long and stedfastly at" the youth. An unavoidable conflict is announced when the Abenaki take to the field again in the coming spring against the English. Tension is then built up throughout the old man's dramatic monologue climaxing in his crucial question whether the English officer could possibly "be ungrateful enough to go over to join thy countrymen, and to lift the hatchet against us?" The explanation, that the old man lost his own son, and that his empathy for the aging father of the Englishman leads him to set the young officer free, solves only one part of the tension. The reader does not learn the reaction of the freed captive.

The most important feature of the text, anticipating the short story, is this open-ended structure. It is retained in all the variants that have surfaced so far, and it enables three potential readings. The transnational and transracial sentimental message conveyed by the story of the captive sent back to his father by a sympathetic captor still mourning his own lost son apparently held considerable appeal on an international scale; this is the reading encouraged by the edited first German version, with its focus on the sentimental impact. This fits the contemporary readings, following the French enlightenment tradition of Louis-Armand Baron de La Hontan, Voltaire, and Chateaubriand, which depicts some—by no means all—"savages" as ennobled by nature and sentiment. This aspect certainly lent credibility to the 1785 claim that the story had originally been translated from the French.

The second reading appealed primarily to colonial British readers. The adoption of captives by Native peoples was not uncommon. In fact, "to gain captives who could replace recently deceased members of their families and communities" was sometimes the rationale behind the participation of individuals in a raid.[14] This very much fits the situation the old man in the story is in, having lost his own son in battle, though the English officer is only referred to as adopted son in the first German translation.

With more than a thousand often autobiographical captivity narratives published, the anonymous author of "Among the Abenakee Savages" had a variety of sources and role models at hand. For example, in 1736 John Gyles published his autobiography *Memoirs of Odd Adventures, Strange Deliverances, &c. in the Captivity of John Gyles, Esq., Commander of the Garrison on St. George's River*. Gyles was abducted from a settlement in Maine in 1689 and grew up among the Mikmaq and Maliseet, two of the nations forming, with the Abenaki, the Wabanaki Confederacy. When released six years later, "he used his linguistic and ethnographic knowledge to establish a niche as a trader, interpreter, diplomat, and military officer on the Massachusetts frontier."[15] He also served in the British army as an interpreter until shortly before his death in 1755. The Mikmaq and Maliseet apparently trusted him.[16] Gyles seems to have been successful in neither betraying his countrymen nor the people that had adopted him—a possibility left open at the end of the text at hand. Another redeemed captive, Joseph Louis Gill, turned his back on the English, married an Abenaki woman and eventually served as a "white chief."[17] These are two of the possibilities arising from the captivity situation at the end of the text at hand as well, but there is, as stated before, no clear resolution.

The third reading is the most important one for the purposes of this collection, since this reading is specifically American; its potential arises from the political situation of 1775. Contemporary readers were likely to have been aware of the historical details and implications of the text. The *Royal American Magazine* commenced publication during a time of unrest: While the title seems to indicate a loyalist position, many of the articles were clearly calculated to criticize the British and colonial governments, and to afford aid and comfort to the rebels. Radical patriot propaganda can be found in every issue of the magazine. This attitude was supported by political cartoons drawn by Paul Revere, who was to become known as one of the most dedicated patriots in the American Revolution.[18] One of his cartoons, published in June 1774, thematized the dispute over the taxation of tea—on December 16, 1773 a group of Bostonians disguised as Native Americans destroyed a shipment of tea in Boston harbor.[19] The importance of this action for the text at hand lies in the interpretation of the use of Native American dress, not so much as a disguise but as an assumption of a visibly "Native American" attitude, influenced by the belief in the enlightened noble savage and symbolizing the colonists' fight for liberal ideals.[20]

Given this background, the publication of "Adventure of a Young English Officer Among the Abenakee Savages" in the penultimate issue of the *Royal American Magazine* before the outbreak of open hostilities at Lexington and Concord in April 1775 takes on an additional meaning, different from both the sentimental and the captivity aspects. As Jack B. Moore noted, the "Indian in much early fiction is no Indian but the well-known white man painted red."[21] The most famous contemporary example of a Native American adopted by the patriot propaganda against the British was arguably the Mingo (Shawnee) chief Logan who lost his family at the hands of an English officer, and whose acts of revenge could therefore be blamed on an incompetent colonial administration.[22] He and other ennobled savages doubled as American colonial figures. From this perspective we can clearly view the old Abenaki in the story at hand, who treats the captive English youth with compassion.

Against the background of impending hostilities in 1775, the conflict in the story is symbolically between England and America rather than between the English and some Native Americans. The (Native) American, in control of the English officer, treats him with nobility and does not take advantage of his position:

> the old man, . . . with signs of peace, took the officer by the hand, after removing his apprehensions by friendly gestures, and carried him home with him to his hut. There he treated him with great humanity and gentleness.

The relation between the Native American and the English youth in some ways parallels the discrepancy of the situation in which a number of British colonial officers found themselves in 1775. In many cases having grown up, or at least having learned their life skills in North America, they found themselves confronted with the question of which side they wanted to be on in the coming conflict.

The originally sentimental storyline, read in the new historical context, constructs the conflict as the result of a difference between the British and the Americans, which appears as a difference between countries. A loyalist would probably have denied this difference; within the rearticulated story, however, it is impossible to solve the problem of the young officer without alienating one or the other group in the impending conflict.

Unity of effect, in the sense that the reader is forced to respond to the emotional impact of the story, is facilitated by the fact that the story features only unnamed characters, enabling the readers of 1775 to relate the English officer's experience to their own (political) situation. Given the political background of Boston in 1775, many colonists found themselves in a similar predicament, having to decide which side they wanted to be on. Unity of effect is further enhanced through the handling of perspective. Because of the dialogue, the reader is invited to take the perspective of the old man; yet simultaneously identification is of course suggested with the English officer on whose ability to find a—seemingly impossible— solution, or compromise, between betraying either his fellow countrymen or his American benefactor, his very life may depend. The reprint of the story in Boston in 1775, in a politically charged situation, imbues the text— because of its open structure—with a politically charged meaning that allows for a re-classification of an originally French magazine text as an early American short story.

Aynur Erdogan, Philipp Fidler

Notes

[1] More commonly spelled *Abenaki*, sometimes also referred to as "St. Francis Abenaki": one of the five indigenous peoples forming the Wabanaki Confederacy, living in Southeastern Quebec.
[2] Preface, *Royal American Magazine* 1 (June, 1774): n. p.
[3] Preface, *Royal American Magazine* 1, Suppl. 1 (1774): n. p.

[4] Presumably the French and Indian War (1755–1763) in which the Abenaki were allied with the French.

[5] thought

[6] An English league is approximately 3 miles. The surprising distance of 600 miles is probably correct: The so-called "war-paths" extended from the indigenous settlements in French Canada through New York State and as far as Massachusetts.

[7] Anon., "Aventure d'un jeune Officier Anglois chez les Sauvages Abenakis; tirée de Memoires particuliers," *Gazette littéraire de l'Europe* 5 [Supplément du dimanche 3 février] (1765): 230–33.

[8] Jean-François de Saint-Lambert, "L'Abenaki," *Contes Americains*, ed. Roger Little (Exeter: U of Exeter P, 1997): 3–5.

[9] Anon., "Adventure of the English Officer Among the Abenakee Savages," *The Gentleman's Magazine* 35 (March 1765): 111–12.

[10] Anon., "Ruehrende Anecdote von einem Wilden," *Hamburgisches Journal* 2 (December, 1765): 1049–51.

[11] Anon., "Begebenheiten eines jungen Englischen Officiers unter den Abenakies," *Hannoverisches Magazin* 4 (1766): 9–14.

[12] Anon., "Adventure of a Young English Officer Among the Abenakee Savages," *Bickerstaff's Boston Almanack, For the Year of our Lord 1768* 1 (1767): n. p. Sachem is an anglicized Eastern Algonquian term for a chief or leader.

[13] Anon., "Adventure of the English Officer Among the Abenakee Savages," *The Royal American Magazine, or Universal Repository of Instruction and Amusement* 2 (February, 1775): 59–61.

[14] Timothy J. Shannon, "War, Diplomacy and Culture," *Cultures in Conflict: The Seven Years' War in North America*, ed. Warren R. Hofstra (Lanham: Rowman & Littlefield, 2007): 81.

[15] Pauline Turner Strong, *Captive Selves, Captivating Others: The Politics and Poetics of Colonial American Captivity Narratives* (Boulder: Westview P, 1999): 166.

[16] Strong, 166.

[17] Strong, 167.

[18] Cf. Frank Luther Mott, *A History of American Magazines: 1741–1850* (Cambridge, MA: Harvard UP, 1957): 84–86.

[19] David L. Ammerman, "The Tea Crisis and its Consequences, through 1775," *A Companion to the American Revolution*, eds. Jack P. Greene and J. R. Pole (Malden, MA: Blackwell, 2000): 195–97.

[20] Cf. Philipp J. Deloria, *Playing Indian* (New Haven: Yale UP, 1998): 7.

[21] Jack B. Moore, *Native Elements in American Magazine Short Fiction: 1741–1800*, diss. U of North Carolina 1963: 11.

[22] Wolfgang Hochbruck, *I Have Spoken: Darstellung und ideologische Funktion indianischer Mündlichkeit in der nordamerikanischen Literatur,* diss. U Tübingen 1991. Tübingen: Narr, 1991: 90.

The Desperate Negroe

Anonymous (Rev. James Ramsay)

"The Desperate Negroe" is located within the sphere of anti-slavery discourse, which includes the political rhetoric of pamphlets, oratory, and essays, as well as autobiographical accounts, and of course fiction. The story presented here is American in that it anticipates characteristic features of the American slave narrative which reached its heyday in the 1840s–60s with narratives such as Frederick Douglass' A Narrative of the Life of Frederick Douglass, An American Slave *(1845)*, Harriet Beecher Stowe's Uncle Tom's Cabin *(1852), and Harriet Ann Jacobs'* Incidents in the Life of a Slave Girl *(1861)*.

However, the story was not originally published in the U.S. It seems to have been written originally by Reverend James Ramsay, an important British abolitionist of the time. Ramsay first encountered the cruelty of slavery during his short naval career when he came into contact with a slave ship infested with the plague. Shortly afterward, he became a minister and set off to work on the Caribbean island of St. Kitts. His political engagement for the benefit of the slaves there aroused the opposition of planters who eventually forced him to return to Britain after fifteen years. There, he published several works on the issue of slavery, most notably "An Essay on the Treatment and Conversion of African Slaves in the British Sugar Colonie." The story of "The Desperate Negroe" is part of this essay.[1]

The first American edition of the story was published in Boston in 1793 in The Massachusetts Magazine, or Weekly Museum of Knowledge and Rational Entertainment. *Frank L. Mott regarded this magazine "one of the best in which to study the early development of the American Short Story."[2] Also, the "Massachusetts Magazine published [...] at least one piece of native fiction for every issue."[3] By the time "The Desperate Negroe" was published, W. Weld and William Greenough had taken over the editorship of the magazine from Isaiah Thomas and Ebenezer T. Andrews, yet without effecting any significant changes on the content level. Of the American magazines of the period,* The Massachusetts Magazine *was probably the one with the greatest breadth, publishing news of the world (gazette) as well as articles on history, politics, music, housekeeping, family, and religion.*

The main character in the story is called Quashi, and the fact that this name was originally found among Jamaican slaves and that the story first appeared in an essay about slavery in the British sugar colonies, suggests that the setting of the story is a plantation in the West Indies. However, within the new cultural context of the Massachusetts publication in 1793, American readers would most likely have located the story in their own country. By 1793 the question of slavery had become an important domestic issue, and Massachusetts, one of the first states to abolish slavery, became a stronghold of the abolitionist movement in the antebellum period. Naturally, questions of slavery and plantation life received great interest in the state.

The Desperate Negroe

QUASHI was brought up in the family with his master, as his play fellow, from his childhood.[4] Being a lad of towardly parts, he rose to be driver, or black overseer, under his master, when the plantation fell to him by succession.[5] He retained for his master the tenderness that he had felt in childhood for his playmate; and the respect with which the relation of master inspired him, was softened by the affection which the remembrance of their boyish intimacy kept alive in his breast. He had no separate interest of his own; and in his master's absence redoubled his diligence, that his affairs might receive no injury from it. In short, here was the most delicate, yet most strong, and seemingly indissoluble tie, that could bind master and slave together.

Though the master had judgment to know when he was well served, and policy to reward good behaviour, he was inexorable when a fault was commited; and when there was but an apparent cause of suspicion, he was apt to let prejudice usurp the place of proof. Quashi could not exculpate himself to his satisfaction, for something done contrary to the discipline on the plantation; and was threatened with the ignominious punishment of the cart whip, and he knew his master too well, to doubt of the performance of his promise.[6]

A negroe, who was grown up to manhood, without undergoing a solemn cart whipping (as some by good chance will, especially if distinguished by any accomplishment among his fellows) takes pride in what he calls the smoothness of his skin, its being unraised by the whip; and he would be at more pains, and use more diligence to escape such cart whipping, than many of our lower sort would use to shun the gallows. It is not uncommon for a sober good negroe to stab himself mortally, because some boy overseer has flogged him for what he reckoned a trifle, or for his caprice, or threatened him with a flogging, when he thought he did not deserve it. Quashi dreaded this mortal wound to his honour, and slipt away unnoticed, with a view to avoid it.

It is usual for slaves, who expect to be punished for their own fault, or their master's caprice, to go to some friend of their master's, and beg him to carry them home, and mediate for them.[7] This is found to be so useful, that humane masters are glad of the pretence of such mediation, and will secretly procure it, to avoid the necessity of punishing for trifles; it otherwise not being prudent to pass over without correction, a fault once taken notice of; while, by this method, an appearance of authority and discipline is kept up, without the severity of it. Quashi therefore withdrew, resolved to shelter himself, and save the glossy honours of his skin, under favour of this custom, till he had an opportunity of applying to an advocate. He lurked among his master's negroe huts; and his fellow slaves had too much honour, and too great a regard for him, to betray to their master the place of his retreat. Indeed, it is hardly possible in any case, to get one slave to inform against another; so much more honour have they than Europeans of low condition.[8]

The following day a feast was kept, on account of his master's nephew then coming of age; amidst the good humour of which, Quashi hoped to succeed in his application: but before he could execute his design, perhaps just as he was setting out to go and solicit his mediation, his master, while walking among his fields, fell in with him. Quashi, on discovering him, ran off, and the master, who was a robust man, pursued him. A stone or a clod, tripped Quashi up, just as the other reached out his hand to seize him. They fell together, and wrestled for the mastery; for Quashi also was a stout man, and the elevation of his mind added vigour to his arm. At last, after a severe struggle, in which each had been several times uppermost, Quashi got firmly seated on his master's breast, now panting and out of breath; and with his weight, his thighs, and one hand, secured him motionless. He then drew out a sharp knife, and while the other lay in dreadful expectation, helpless, and shrinking into himself, he thus addressed him: "Master, I was bred up with you from a child; I was your playmate when a boy; I have loved you as myself; your interest has been my study; I am innocent of the cause of your suspicion; had I been guilty, my attachment to you might have pleaded for me. Yet, you have condemned me to a punishment, of which I must ever have borne the disgraceful marks; thus only can I avoid them." With these words he drew the knife with all his strength across his own throat, and fell down dead without a groan, on his master, bathing him in his blood.

Critical Commentary

Unlike other stories in this volume, "The Desperate Negroe" has already attracted some scholarly attention. Moore calls the story one of the more noteworthy examples of early American magazine fiction in his dissertation and also mentions it in an article dealing with depictions of blacks in the same publishing context.[9] More recently, John Saillant has speculated about same-sex eroticism within the narrative.[10] An independent analysis of the story itself, however, has not been attempted.

Though evidently not as skillfully constructed as later texts by Hawthorne, Melville, and Poe, "The Desperate Negroe" succeeds in using irony and ambiguity to create a dense narrative. Also, there is a certain proximity to contemporary political rhetoric, resulting in a noticeable "unity of effect." Unlike most magazine fiction of the time, "The Desperate Negroe" makes very economic use of mimetic features. The story is related by an authorial narrator who reveals himself as such in the phrase "than many of *our* lower sort would use to shun the gallows" (emphasis added). Handling of time is very basic. The story-time encompasses two days, with Quashi escaping into the shelter of the "negroe huts" on the first day and his struggle with master and eventual suicide on the second.

The plot, though not elaborate, is handled skillfully. For example, the use of retarding descriptions about the general practice and circumstances on plantations creates an arch of suspense, once the basic conflict is established. The eventual suicide of Quashi is foreshadowed in the sentence, "It is not uncommon for a sober good negroe to stab himself mortally, because some boy overseer has flogged him for what he reckoned a trifle, or for his caprice, or threatened him with a flogging, when he thought he did not deserve it." The ending of the story refrains from making a clear moral statement. Instead, the imagery leaves an ambiguous impression. On the one hand, Quashi seems to preserve his physical and moral integrity by killing himself. On the other hand, the very act of suicide would have been considered a grave sin in the eyes of Puritan American society in the late 18th century. The conflict remains unresolved. In this light, the title "The *Desperate* Negroe" is adequatly chosen because the circumstances of plantation life leave Quashi with no options; not even his last resort can succeed to grant him freedom.

Most emphasis of the story is placed on characterization. Quashi, the protagonist, is sentimentalized as having "no separate interest of his own," possessing "honour" and "diligence" in the highest degree. He exhibits physical beauty in the form of "the glossy honours of his skin," thus contradicting the common pro-slavery argument of the physical inferiority and brute-like appearance of the African. His depiction reaches its pinnacle with the desperate speech toward the end of the narrative. The slave's personal integrity and moral superiority is contrasted by the foil character of his nameless master, who is "apt to let prejudice usurp the place of proof" and who displays "caprice" rather than humanity. This depiction of Quashi is very much in accordance with the general portrayal of Africans in early American magazine fiction as described by Moore.[11] Nonetheless, characterization in "The Desperate Negroe" stretches far beyond the use of stock characters.

The fact that Quashi has a name, indeed is the only character in the story that is given one, is an indication of a degree of individuation, even though the name is, like most names in the stories of the late 18th century, generic. It is emphasized by the author's opening of the narrative with his name, printed in capital letters. Moreover, Quashi is an African name, originating from the Akan language of Ghana. This makes him different from literary characters such as "Friday" and even "Uncle Tom," since he is apparently not subject to naming by his white masters. Quashi retains at least part of his original identity.

Orlando Patterson points out that "Quashee" became a stock name and image of a specifically Jamaican slave type, "a general pattern that has been recognized all over the New World" with features like dishonesty, distrustfulness, laziness, caprice, and irresponsibility.[12] These qualities stand in direct opposition to those attributed to the character in the story. This would either make the choice of name consciously ironic, or else the name had not yet taken on the range of connotations noted by Patterson.

The description of the characterization in "The Desperate Negroe" reveals the general thrust of the text. There is a clear political impetus to the story, situating it within the larger context of the abolitionist movement, which was gathering strength at the time. Though a work of fiction, it makes use of some of the standard elements of anti-slavery rhetoric; in fact, "The Desperate Negroe" is a good example of the interface between fictional and non-fictional narration, where the story of the character's fictionalized and individualized fate uses strategies of political rhetoric while echoing arguments of "factual" discourse.

As has been pointed out, the depiction of Quashi in many ways follows the general image of slaves in similar texts. Since they were published in New England magazines, these texts took a clearly abolitionist stance. "Nearly all the stories are highly critical of slavery as an immoral and brutalizing institution," and they also present "the Negro as an attractive, decent, sometimes violent sometimes heroic human being."[13] These are all important elements of characterization in the case of Quashi.

Likewise, contrasting virtuous slave and reckless planter is a common device in this respect. In "The Desperate Negroe" this contrast is not limited to the character level, but extends to the whole institution of slavery. The narrator repeatedly engages in general remarks about the two groups. The slaves, represented by the concept of "a sober good negroe," have "much more honour . . . than Europeans of low condition" and will "use more diligence to escape [a] cart whipping, than many of our lower sort would use to shun the gallows." Here, class and race divisions are regarded as separate and completely independent from each other, a quite modern notion for the time of the original publication of the story, and a direct challenge to the basis of much pro-slavery argumentation.

The most subtle contradiction to the slaveholders' rationale is directed against the idea that slavery provides an improvement of the condition of Africans, based on the belief that they would not be able to lead a civilized life unless controlled and directed by white leadership. This concept is subverted in two ways. The first regards the apparent charity of the plantation microcosm. In "The Desperate Negroe," ideal conditions seem to be provided: Quashi is in a privileged position, as the "black overseer," and a "seemingly indissoluble tie" connects him to his master. He works hard and has "no separate interest of his own," the master has "judgment to know when he [is] well served, and policy to reward good behaviour." Yet by the end of the story, Quashi is left with suicide as the only way out of his despair. Not even the "useful" practice of mediation through a neighbor, which a "humane" master would welcome, can prevent this outcome. In the context of the story, adjectives and adverbs like these sound ironic: The institution of slavery is everything but "useful" for, or "humane" toward, its subjects.

The second way in which the idea of a need for white leadership is negated is the portrayal of the slave community itself. The reader gets telling information about the "master's negroe huts," which are described as forming an intact community within the society of the plantation, able to function at least partly according to their own rules. Otherwise, it would not be possible for Quashi to hide there from his master. The fact that the other slaves keep the fugitive hidden against the will of the master enhances this impression. Of course, such behavior might also be interpreted in a negative way, likening it to a sort of criminal complot. But the signals given in the text clearly identify it as motivated by "honour" rather than otherwise. If a community can retain such a close-knit bond under such extreme circumstances, the claim of a negro's incapability to lead a civilized lifestyle of his own cannot possibly be upheld.

The last, and arguably most important, concept of pro-slavery discourse attacked in "The Desperate Negroe" is that of the white man's natural superiority. When the two antagonists wrestle for "mastery" at the end of the narrative, this expression is apparently chosen with deliberation. Their struggle is not only about physical supremacy, but figuratively speaking also about personal and moral superiority. The development of the story to this point has left little doubt that Quashi is the one who will win this fight—and he does. The question remains as to why Quashi does not kill his master rather than committing suicide.

This is not the kind of sudden death that ends other examples of American magazine fiction from the same period, apparently in order to stay within the allotted printing space.[14] This is unlikely also because the original British publishing context would have allowed for more space. A more plausible explanation is that Quashi's death is necessary: Had he used his momentous position of power to gain freedom, this act would have been regarded as a crime in the eyes of contemporary society. Abolitionism had not yet reached its later, more radical form, calling for the instant liberation of all slaves.[15] Even liberal thinkers of the late 18th century would not have condoned the killing of a planter by one of his slaves. Quashi's suicide, however, preserves his dignity, and the fight between Quashi and his master anticipates a motif more consistently realized in *A Narrative of the Life of Frederick Douglass* half a century later. There, the protagonist wins a fight against his master, refusing to accept oppression by a man who is his intellectual and physical inferior.[16]

As far as the genre is concerned, the text reprinted here was originally called an anecdote, possibly because of its brevity, though this term itself does not foreclose a different classification. At first glance, the sudden turn at the end may appear anecdotal, but a closer reading shows that the outcome is foreshadowed and can be anticipated by the attentive reader. Furthermore, there is too much elaboration to uphold a strict moral or point that is typical for the anecdote. This elaboration does not, however, take on the episodic style of the tale.

A classification as character sketch is ruled out by the generic name and the absence of any deeper individuation. More likely the depiction of "The Desperate Negroe" is an exemplum, with figures in the text representing larger ideas and institutions. Other than the exemplum in the sermonic tradition, however, the story at least in the form in which it (re-)appeared in *The Massachusetts Magazine* refrains from giving a definite moral, leaving the reader with an ambiguous ending instead.

This ending ties in with other textual strategies anticipating the allusive, and often ironic, technique of the short story. The master does not win the fight for "mastery," the "seemingly indissoluble tie" that connects planter and slave at the beginning turns out to be everything but beneficial. For Quashi, this tie is a much more literal one. He is chained to the institution of slavery and the relationship between him and his former playfellow is a highly vertical one. Readers inclined to blame the master for Quashi's fate, however, are also given signals portraying his figure in a somewhat positive light as one who has "judgment" and rewards "good behaviour." It is left to the reader to decide whether these statements are mere irony. Another reading might seek the fault not on the character level but in the institution of slavery itself. Equally ambiguous is the ending, which refrains from glorifying Quashi. His suicide is not a heroic act of martyrdom, but a sign of desperation. Even in this, his integrity is not fully preserved, considering the religious norms of Puritan society.

The resulting lack of clarity and the absence of an explicit message call for a careful reading. There are moments of foreshadowing in the text, such as the passage introducing the motif of suicide, or statements such as the one about the "indissoluble tie" between Quashi and his master. Confronted and subverted in the course of the story, they call for a re-reading, and reinterpretation, of "The Desperate Negroe"—yet another characteristic of later short stories by such writers as Hawthorne and Poe.

Despite the many ambiguities within the text, it works toward a single effect. The narrative fictionalizes arguments of abolitionism, directed at attacking the institution of slavery. In their fictionalized form, however, they display varying degrees of subtlety, leaving it to the reader's interpretation to draw conclusions. Hence, a unity of effect is achieved instead of the didactic presentation of an explicit moral statement. This reflects the paradigm shift that led away from monodirectional cultures of meaning and toward literary ambiguities, as described in the Introduction to this volume.

The publication history at first glance contradicts a classification as *American*, but it should be noted that even in its original form, "The Desperate Negroe" contained a degree of transnationality: set on a sugar plantation in the colonies, and focusing on the figure of Quashi, it stresses elements of West Indian cultural history. The crucial point for the present study, however, is the transition into the new American publishing context. The reader-oriented approach, which the selection in this volume is based upon, allows for a classification of the text as American, for a new and distinctly American meaning emerges from the text as a result of its changed environment and readership.

Jörg Binder, Axel Bohmann

Notes

[1] James Ramsay, *An Essay on the Treatment and Conversion of African Slaves in the British Sugar Colonies* (London: J. Phillips, 1784): 248–53.

[2] Frank Luther Mott, *A History of American Magazines: 1741–1850* (Cambridge, MA: Harvard UP, 1957): 109.

[3] Jack B. Moore, *Native Elements in American Magazine Short Fiction: 1741–1800,* diss. U of North Carolina 1963: 245.

[4] The name "Quashee" can be traced to the Akan language of Ghana, where it is common for children to be named after the day on which they are born. This tradition was carried on by Jamaican slaves of Ghanaian descent. Quashee is the name for a male born on a Sunday. The name came to be a denotation of the stereotypical slave of Jamaica and the entire New World. Also, the reference to Quashi and his master having been playfellows in their childhood might be an indication that Quashi was his later master's half-brother. Sexual relationships between planters and female slaves were not uncommon, and this practice often resulted in slave-holders having illegitimate children. These children were hardly ever acknowledged, but sometimes they received better treatment than regular slave children, such as Quashi is described as having experienced in his childhood.

[5] Overseers existed on nearly every farm or plantation with more than 30 slaves. They were employed to relieve the planters, and spent almost all of their time on the plantation to control the slaves' work. The job was considered very important as production and profit depended on the discipline. If the overseer was too soft, the slaves would not work properly. If the overseer was too brutal, the planter would make him responsible for damage to his property.

[6] Whipping was the most common punishment in the time of slavery. Slaves were usually punished for arguing, fighting, stealing, and drunkenness. Often, slaves received whippings of more than 100 lashes.

[7] This practice seems to grant a surprisingly high amount of freedom to the slave and its alleged prevalence sounds questionable to the modern reader. Yet, James Ramsay, the original author of the story, had first-hand insight into plantation life in the West Indies.

[8] Slaves usually lived in their own assembly of small, often self-built cabins, on the plantation. The huts were sometimes augmented by a kitchen and a laundry cabin. A few slave quarters had the size of small villages and included a church or a chapel. In many cases, slaves provided for themselves with small gardens; others were provided for by their masters.

[9] Jack B. Moore, "Images of the Negro in Early American Short Fiction," *Mississippi Quarterly: A Journal of Southern Culture* 22 (1969): 47–58.

[10] John Saillant, "The Black Body Erotic and the Republican Body Politic, 1790–1820," *Journal of the History of Sexuality* 5.3 (1995): 403–28.

[11] Moore, *Images of the Negro*, 47–57.

[12] Orland Patterson, *The Sociology of Slavery: An Analysis of the Origins, Development and Structure of Negro Slave Society in Jamaica* (Rutherford: Fairleigh Dickinson UP, 1975): 174.

[13] Moore, *Images of the Negro*, 50, 57.

[14] See, for example, the story "Yonora" in this collection.

[15] See, David L. Lightner, *Slavery and the Commerce Power: How the Struggle against the Interstate Slave Trade led to the Civil War* (New Haven: Yale UP, 2006): 57–64.

[16] Frederick Douglass, *Narrative of the Life of Frederick Douglass, An American Slave, Written by Himself*, ed. David W. Blight (Boston: Bedford Books of St. Martin's P, 1993): 71–94.

Yonora
An American Indian Tale
Melpomene

The author of "Yonora" is known to the modern reader only by her pen name Melpomene. Mixing facts from the autobiographical as well as historical accounts of the French nobleman Antoine Simon Le Page du Pratz with other sources and names, and somewhat incongruously adding a number of stock elements of sentimental fiction, she created what seems to have been a piece of original American fiction. Some doubts remain, since the sources used for "Yonora" highlight a French language background. In any case, the story is interesting and must have appealed to contemporary readers for being a piece of clearly American historical short prose fiction. "American" is used here in an encompassing sense that covers all inhabitants of the continent, European as well as indigenous.

The story was published in the first issue of the South Carolina Weekly Museum *in January 1797. This magazine, printed by W. P. Harrison & Co. and edited by T. P. Bowen, appeared semi-annually, until it was discontinued in July 1798. Its contents were a miscellany of tales, poetry, and essays on foreign and domestic politics. Published in Charleston, it was the first and only magazine published south of Baltimore in the 18th century.*

Yonora: An American Indian Tale

How must the aged parent sigh and drop affliction's tear—how oft the sympathy of the grey haired sire, mourn the sad fate of his child, and the heart strings of maternal affection to be severed? Alas! the tale of human woes already presents a distressing catalogue, and the history of Yonora adds another trait to the calamitous picture.

The discovery of America has expanded the wings of liberty, wasted its effulgence to the most distant extremities of the earth, and ameliorated the situation of all mankind—the whole human race are progressing by rapid strides to the enjoyment of the blessings which owe their birth to this event; but while we view this picture with all the emotions of a Philanthropic heart, and feel the most exquisite sensations of pleasure at the recital, candor must turn the medal and reverse the scene; truth must establish this maxim, that there is no page of the history of human life, which is not stained by the relation of some woeful tale. Truth will say, here valor bled; there the noble mind was made to brook an ignominious fate; here beauty suffered by the ruffian hand; there virtue bowed her head to vice. The history of America, like that of all other nations contains a sombre side, like them acknowledges the weakness of man, and that perfect happiness is inconsistent with his nature. In it, as in others, the eye which traces the page of its story must drop a tear of humanity. We may rank among these distressing circumstances, the wars which have so frequently existed between the Whites and the Aborigines of the soil.

The Ichitimachas were a nation of Indians in North America, living upon the banks of the Mississippi and bordering upon the colony of Louisiana.[1] Of this nation was Logan and the lovely Yonora his daughter, who makes the subject of this story, which will draw a sigh from the least feeling heart, if a sigh is due where all that is virtuous, all that is most beautiful, suffers the rude shock of misfortune. Logan was one of the principal warriors of his nation, he sat in council and was a leader in their debates, and by the marriage of his daughter with the monarch of the Ichitimachas was allied to the throne: from his valor, his abilities, and his connections, he was exalted to the most dignified posts of honor, that the nature of the government afforded: to the enjoyment of those, Logan found in his bosom that of an affectionate wife, who tempered the severity of life, to which we are all destined in a greater or lesser degree. When the rude blasts of war raged and the fated arrow pierced the breast of Logan, her heart throbbed with his—she participated in his pain—she applied the balm to his wounds, and only when nature and her cares had done away their stings, did she cease to feel with him, their anguish. By this affectionate woman, Logan had two daughters; the eldest of whom was called, by the sovereign of the nation, to participate in the honors of the throne—the younger was the fair Yonora, who possessed every endearing quality, that can adorn the sex, and added to the most exquisite natural beauty, all the improvements that the state of society in which she lived, could afford. Thus surrounded, Logan had arrived at the zenith of human happiness; but the Gods, whose wisdom is sometimes impenetrable to human eye, wherefore we must not censure, determined to check his career and subject him to the bitterest of human miseries.

The French having settled the colony of Louisiana, the missionaries of that nation, zealous for the extension of their religion, spread themselves among the Indians, with a view of converting them to the Christian faith and making proselytes of them to their religion.[2] The Indians in many instances did not like this description of people, although they silently submitted to their dictates—the nature of their religion being too morose and severe to the genius of a barbarous people. One of the Ichitimachas, perhaps more averse to their domination than the rest, and guided by a vicious heart, perpetrated an act on one of those missionaries which involved their nation in a long and bloody war with the colony of Louisiana, then quite an infant state.[3] M. de St. Come was the unhappy person who went to the house of this man, intending to rest on his hospitality, for a nights entertainment; and in the mean time to fulfil the functions of his mission by instilling the principles of his religion into the mind of his host—he thought himself in security—but the event shows in how melancholy a degree he was mistaken—he fell a victim to some unaccountable passion which agitated the breast of the Indian, who thereby brought down the vengeance of the French upon his nation, who, moved by the spirit of revenge made war with as much ferocity upon them, as the barbarous manners and customs of the Indians lead them to do on the Whites.

Oft had the laurel crowned the brow of Logan. Oft had the enemies of his country felt the weight of his attack, and acknowledged the valor of his mind—he was now called from these scenes of felicity which we have described, to act a part in the contest, to protect his country from the ravages of its enemies, and their wives and children from captivity and death.

The war had been carried on for some time with alternate success. Sometimes victory displayed its banner on the side of Logan, at others on the side of the Whites. Logan had a faithful friend who attended him in these adventures, who had been his close companion from infancy, and who now fought by his side, and often averted the uplifted weapon which aimed at his life. Logan, feeling all the emotions of a generous and valiant soul, had often repaid the favour and laid his friend under similar obligations to him but one day less happy than the rest, he received the fatal arrow which checked the current of life, deprived Logan of a firm and faithful friend and the Ichitimachas of a brave warrior. He died—and had only time to tell his friend to be a father to his son, the only offspring of his blood, who was to continue to posterity his fame and his valor; and in leaving his son under the care of Logan he fully compensated the youth for the loss he sustained in his death: he was indeed a father to him, and the ties of nature could not have more firmly cemented his attachment, than those of friendship did. This youth whose name was Piomingo was conspicuous for all the virtues of his father, and added to them, the most graceful person, that can be conceived. He had been in the habit of intimacy with Yonora from their tender years—and the unfortunate fate of his father tightened the bands of their friendship—Logan esteeming the youth for his amiable qualities, was pleased with the idea of effecting a union betwixt them—he suggested the idea, and it succeeded so far as to meet their perfect approbation—he not only aided the spark which already struggled for birth, but laid the foundation of a lasting but unfortunate interchange of affections: they cherished it with all the zeal of youth, and lived on each idea as if it measured the last moment of time—they only waited for the conclusion of the war to consummate their nuptials—that war which alas! was to blast every hope, and put it beyond, even the power of the Gods, to tye the hymeneal cord.

While the warriors of the Ichitimachas were engaged at a distance from their habitations in carrying on the war, while they swam in blood and were surrounded with victory—the French fell behind them, entered their towns, laid them in ashes and carried away their wives and children, captives.

Logan and his companions hearing of this disaster, hastened to relieve their fortune and their fame—and if possible, to redeem at the price of their blood, their wives and children from captivity. They attained the object of their exertions; but, while each saw his offspring and his wife, once more in his arms, Logan alone mourned the loss of his—he who was but yesterday the happiest mortal on whom the sun shed his ray, now drank deep of the stream of affliction.

Piomingo at this time fought in the battles of his country, he occupied the place of his deceased parent, in supporting and defending his adopted sire—he too, unhappy youth, had to mourn, in the daughter of Logan, the loss of the dear object of his desires—he prayed to the Gods to make her happy and bring her again to her lover's arms—he glutted with revenge and made the earth to flow with the blood of his enemies: but it brought not Yonora to his view, nor put him in the enjoyment of her charms—he pined in despair, he thought she was no more and lost the hope of again embracing his love, that fond hope so pleasing to his thoughts vanished, and in its exit doubled the anguish of his pains. Yonora in the mean time was labouring under the lash of servitude, her mind was tortured with anxiety for the fate of Piomingo. She knew not, if like her, his haughty and soaring mind was bowed beneath the yoke of servitude and oppression, or if the dart of death had deprived him of the vital spark.

The war continued with all its fury, during the long space of twelve years, when the Ichitimachas, having lost their bravest warriors in the field of battle, had their fields ruined, and their towns laid in ashes, sought peace at the hands of the whites: the latter prescribed as the condition on which it would be granted, that they should deliver the head of the murderer of the Missionary, who had by that act been the author of those ruinous consequences, which we have contemplated. A peace on this condition was concluded, and the time drew on, when they were to smoke the Calamut of peace together, and with it give their mutual grievances to the winds.[4] It arrived and in the progress of the ceremony the orator of the embassy delivered the following speech:

"Oh! that sun is fine today, in comparison with what it was when you were incensed against us. But a wicked man is dangerous—you know that one only perpetrated the crime, which has made so many of our bravest warriors fall—there remains with us now none but the old women and children—you have demanded the head of the murderer, as the condition of peace—we have brought it to you—that old warrior alone of our nation dared to encounter and kill him; but be not surprised, for he has always been a good man and a brave warrior—he is the parent of our sovereign, and weeps day and night because his wife and his child are no more since the commencement of this fatal war—but he is content and so am I, because he hath killed thy enemy. Formerly the sun was red, the roads were full of briers and thorns, the clouds were black and the rivers were tainted with our blood, our wives wept without ceasing, and our children cried out with fear; our houses were abandoned and our fields lay uncultivated; the cravings of nature were unsatisfied, and our bare bones were exposed to the rude blasts of the wind: at this day the sun is warm and brilliant, the Heavens are clear, and the clouds are chased away: the roads present that smoothness of peace and the transparent brook reflects our images; the chase returns, our wives dance, and our children leap like the young hinds of the mountain: the hearts of all our nation leaps with joy, because we walk together in the same path and because we are now all Frenchmen. In future the same sun shall enlighten us, we will have no longer but one voice, we will eat together like brothers and that only shall be good which thou callest so."[5]

Judge what were the feelings of Yonora, who was present at the delivery of this speech, and saw in the orator her lover, and in the venerable and valiant chief, who had given peace to his country, her aged sire. Judge how the pulse of filial affection must have beaten, how the heart must have throbbed with the emotions of love, during the continuance of the harangue, which required the strictest silence, the breach of which might have been attended with serious consequences: The now happy Yonora waited in silence the end of the ceremony, when she came to embrace her father and her lover: time had raised furrows in the old man's cheek, and the beauty of Yonora had dwindled to the faint lightnings of the solar ray; but though time had ravaged her fair visage, the instant he saw her he felt she was his daughter, and love, though blind recognized its object—Piomingo ran into her embraces— they to the wonder and amazement of all spectators, who were as yet unacquainted with the circumstances which we have related, remained wholly enveloped in the ecstasy of their joys—they were indeed sweet, but in the same degree they tended to aggravate the ills which hovered over their heads and followed in quick succession.

Yonora was redeemed—the father enjoyed his child, and the lover, as he thought, was nearly in the embraces of his bride—their return to their nation was to complete their happiness; but human foresight is weak and delusive. The book of destination recorded for them another fate.

The Ichitimachas on this occasion only sent a small deputation of their principal warriors to fix definitely their Treaty of amity with the whites: they were at the same time engaged in war with a neighbouring nation against whom it was necessary to be guarded, and therefore they pursued this plan, that they might not divest themselves of the means of defence—but that which gave security to the nation, was fatal to the unfortunate of whom we are speaking. E'er they had journeyed far from the settlements of the whites, and e'er they had enjoyed long the temporary felicity which attended them, they were taken prisoners by their enemies, who hearing of their embassy, had formed the design of intercepting them, and glutting that revenge so characteristic of these barbarous people, and as we see, succeeded but too well in the attempt—Logan and Piomingo bled—Yonora witnessed it, and with their death, the dissolution of all that she esteemed of humanity. She wished to follow them to those regions of bliss, where the winds of nature blow not, nor bring on their pinions the vicissitudes of human life.

She pursued that path, which philosophers have vindicated, which Christians condemn, and which delivered Yonora, at least, from all sublunary pains.

Critical Commentary

What strikes the reader as important right from the start is Melpomene's—or the editor's—insistence on calling "Yonora" *An American Indian Tale*. The story is set long before the American independence, in the *French* colony of Louisiana at the time of a twelve-year war which followed the assassination of a French missionary. This fact draws attention to the territorial approach to the meaning of *America* taken by the editors of the *South Carolina Weekly Museum*, years before the *Monroe Doctrine*, to include all of North America. Still, Melpomene appears to have felt that her sources were somewhat lacking in regional interest since she introduces, out of chronology and thousands of miles from his historical whereabouts, the figure of Logan, whose famous speech at the conclusion of Lord Dunmore's War was a favorite of American propagandists during the War of Independence. Hailed by Thomas Jefferson as comparable to the orations of Cicero and Demosthenes, his rhetorical style and tone—or at least its English rendition—can be detected behind the rhetoric of Logan and Piomingo.

The ambition to present *An American Indian Tale* not just in the conventional sentimental format but as an early piece of historical fiction, is marred by a number of formal problems and incongruencies. Some of them are clearly deficiencies in structure and style, some may have to do with the historic sources used by Melpomene. Among the incongruencies, the first paragraph sticks out: It does not make much sense with respect to the rest of the story. The omniscient narrator's lament for parents losing a child is clearly not what happens in the story. The second paragraph does not fit in with the rest of the story either. The initial celebration of American history is balanced against the history of colonial wars against the indigenous population, but again, there is no concrete relevance for the following text. The general tone and the misinformed content leave the impression that the story in its present form may have been revised by an editor, or by another writer.

The other end of the text also shows one of the classic deficiencies of contemporary short prose fiction: The lengthy rendition of speeches is more than counterbalanced by the disproportional celerity with which the ending is brought on and all central figures are disposed of. A possible impression on the reader is that the author ran out of time, or space: In speeches and reunion, the time of narrating equals narrated time—the ambush, and the deaths of Logan, Yonora's lover Piomingo, and Yonora herself, are told in 21 lines.

Characterization is not a strong point of the story either. Logan is chief of the Ichitimachas and a family man leading a happy life with his wife and two daughters, one of them Yonora. When a Native kills a missionary, the French take revenge, and in the ensuing war Logan loses first his best friend in battle, then his family in a French attack on his village. Yonora survives, but is taken captive, and is restored to her father and lover—the son of Logan's friend—close to what readers of sentimental tales would expect to be the ending. The late introduction of Piomingo in the second third of the text, and his assumption of functions that might equally well have been served by Logan, are surpassed by the unexpected turn when both Logan and Piomingo are killed on their way home after the peace negotiations. Having witnessed their deaths,

Yonora commits suicide. This action ranges within sentimental logic, but readers might speculate whether the ambush and death were not part of an as yet undisclosed source Melpomene used.

The three central figures are developed only to a point. Logan is the typical brave and honorable chief, whereas Piomingo is described stereotypically as "conspicuous for all the virtues of his father" and "most graceful." Considering the fact that the story is named after Yonora, one would presume that her figure at least would have been developed to a certain extent. Still, none of her descriptions go beyond such features as "fair," "lovely" and "beautiful." Nor is she characterized through actions except for her suicide in the end. Also, the title heroine does not get a single line of dialogue in the whole story.

The lack of specifications in setting is probably owed to the necessity of having to stay brief. Beyond the most general statements about Louisiana, there are no references to features of the landscape, or a description of the place where the Chitimacha live, though they would have been available from Le Page du Pratz.

The most outstanding and interesting feature of the story is its apparent adherence to historical accuracy, or at least to its historiographic source. Jack B. Moore does not seem to have been aware of the extent to which Melpomene used historical sources, referring only to its "historical ... probability," and stating that "the conflict between white and red ... is described in almost any book on American history."[6] The most important hint at the sources is in the text itself, footnoting the "genuine speech" ascribed to Piomingo with a reference to the French author Antoine Simon Le Page du Pratz. In his *Histoire de la Louisiane*, du Pratz, who lived with the

Natchez people for several years and who even had a Chitimacha slave woman not unlike the ill-fated Yonora working for him, mentions that shortly before he arrived in Louisiana in 1718, the French had been at war with the Chitimacha. History and story coincide in that du Pratz mentions as the cause of the war the murder of the missionary de St. Come. As a reaction, M. de Biainville (or Bienville) "commandant general of the company" in Louisiana, caused the Chitimachas "to be attacked by several nations in alliance with the French." When the Chitimachas sued for peace, one of the conditions was that the head of St. Come's murderer be handed over.[7]

There are two pieces of circumstantial evidence beyond the two opening paragraphs that suggest a possible French language background for "Yonora." One is another account of the events of 1706–1718, *Fleur de Lys and Calumet*, written originally in French by André Pénicault, who lived in Louisiana close to the Indians during these years. The circumstances of the murder of "M. de St. Cosme, a priest, sleeping on the bank of the Missicipy with the three Frenchmen and one little slave who were with him," is reported in more detail; his murderer is killed in the retaliatory strike, in which M. de St. Denis led a war party of "savages, two hundred men, with ten Frenchmen." Pénicault spoke the Chitimacha language and at least according to his own account initiated the peace talks between French and Indians.[8] Pénicault's greater historical accuracy extends to the spelling of names: the murdered priest's name, given as "St. Come" in du Pratz and in "Yonora," was spelled like in *Fleur de Lys*, "St. Cosme." Jean François Buisson de St. Cosme even left a travelogue of his own.[9]

The second item is even more telling. Piomingo's speech, allegedly from the source quoted by Melpomene, is not part of the English 1774 edition of du Pratz' *History of Louisiana*, in which "The War with the Chitimachas" is covered by a mere handful of paragraphs at the beginning of the sixth chapter. However, the presence of a speech at a peace conference among the thirteen pages of the original *French* edition covering the Chitimacha war (here spelled "Tchitimachas," probably the source of the otherwise inexplicable spelling as "Ichitimachas" in "Yonora") indicates the close relation between the two texts.[10]

There is no name for the Indian speaker, and du Pratz's focus is more on the ceremony called the "calumet of peace." Melpomene also omits parts of the speech, and the translation does not aim at precision, but shows that it needs to be thought of as a dramatizing adaptation—somewhat camouflaged by the claim that the speech at hand was delivered in a "similar case."

Another important detail is the possibility that the author of "Yonora" might have been inspired by the biography of du Pratz' Chitimacha slave, who also was lost to her father and found again at the peace conference: "It was the father of my slave, who had been captured in this war, and he thought that she was dead like her mother: my slave was with the other girls and did not know what to say; I had the opportunity to see her and I saw her at the same time smile and shed tears."[11] This is close to the description of the meeting of Logan and Yonora.

This leaves the presence of the historical Shawnee leader James Logan, and the also historical Chickasaw politician Piomingo in this story warranting an explanation. The historical Tah-Gah-Jute, a.k.a. John or James Logan, lived from 1725–1780. Initially having excellent relations with white settlers in Pennsylvania and the Ohio Territory, these turned into hatred when his family was murdered by a white frontier trader in 1774. Logan went on to become a prominent leader in the following so-called Lord Dunmore's War, eventually refusing to participate in the peace negotiations. It was on this occasion that he gave the famous speech that so impressed Thomas Jefferson, and which made it into numerous anthologies and schoolbooks from its first printing in *The Pennsylvania Journal and Weekly Advertiser* on February 1, 1775.[12]

Yonora's father, albeit fictional, would thus in any case have predated the historical Logan. The inclusion of his name, as well as that of Piomingo, is one of the genuinely Americanizing features of the text. It must have been included to appeal to the intended readership since the Dunmore Treaty had been signed only five years before the printing of "Yonora," so that Logan's name, and his speech, were present in the minds of the readership. That it is not Logan but Piomingo who gets to speak in the story is *not* one of the incongruencies of the text: Piomingo was the driving force behind the Chickasaw policy to side with the American colonists in Virginia against the British in the 1780s. He was still alive when this story was published, but no individual speech of his achieved the popularity of Logan's. His name, however, and his importance as a friend of the Americans were probably as present as Logan's, so that in combination these two brought together, in fiction, a typical American indigene voicing complaints against the colonial administration, and one supporter of the American cause.

The setting in a distinct historical context and the presence of historical personages and actions makes "Yonora" a piece of historical fiction, and an early representative of the genre at that. Whether it is an original piece of American fiction or not, must be left open. Moore points out the general popularity of "the Indian" occupying a "considerable body of fictional matter" of the period. Moore also claims that "Yonora" avoids sentimentality and stereotyping, and that there is a psychological plausibility of the characters.[13] Considering some of the formal and structural deficiencies of the story, this is at least a questionable statement. However, he also points out that there are moments in "Yonora" which distinguish the story from most of the other stories about Indian people. Much of this fiction either focuses on humor or on the noble savage, while "Yonora" treats its topic seriously, and thematizes a colonial conflict.

As for its possible identification as an early short story, "unity of effect" in the sense that Poe had in mind may have been attempted in that the author followed "one pre-established design," but at least as a reader-response category, this does not quite achieve its aim. The incongruous composition, the frequent shifts of focus, and the lack of focus on Yonora herself, make the effect not quite unified. However, there is no evidence of a moral and didactic purpose either, and the sentimental style appears mainly superimposed on a historically factual storyline, enhanced through the use of historical indigenous characters: Though the historical short story had not found its form yet, this story is one of the ancestors of later texts, notably those of James Fenimore Cooper, who used similar techniques of combining historical sources with and personal references of contemporary interest.

Lisa Kühne

Notes

[1] The Ichitimachas were more commonly referred to as *Chitimacha*. To this day they are a federally recognized tribe in Southwest Louisiana.

[2] Louisiana became a French colony in 1699.

[3] The war referred to here is the 12-year war between the French and the Chitimacha (1706–1718).

[4] The *chalumeau*, usually spelled *calumet* in English adaptations, is the legendary peace pipe.

[5] In the original publication, this section is footnoted as follows: *"This speech is genuine and was actually delivered in a similar case. It is taken, with some of the circumstances of this story, from an obscure history of Louisiana, in French par M. de le Page Du Pratz. Vol. I."*

[6] Jack B. Moore, *Native Elements in American Magazine Short Fiction: 1741–1800*, diss. U of North Carolina 1963: 18.

[7] Antoine Simon Le Page du Pratz, *Histoire de la Louisiane* (Paris: De Bure, La Veuve et Lambert, 1758). Translated as *The History of Louisiana, or of the Western Parts of Virginia and Carolina*, ed. Joseph G. Tregle (Baton Rouge: Louisiana State UP, 1975): 28, 20, 12, 17, 77.

[8] André Pénicault, *Fleur de Lys and Calumet: Being the Pénicaut Narrative of French Adventure in Louisiana*, ed. and trans. Richebourg G. McWilliams (Baton Rouge: Louisiana State UP, 1953): 71, 72, 217.

[9] Jean François Buisson de St. Cosme, *Voyage of St. Cosme. 1698–1699* (Wisconsin: Wisconsin Historical Society, 2003).

[10] The whole seventh chapter, 105–17.

[11] du Pratz, *The History of Louisiana*, 112.

[12] Thomas Jefferson, *Notes on the State of Virginia*, ed. Thomas Perkins Abernethy (New York: Harper, 1964): 60. Wolfgang Hochbruck, *I Have Spoken: Darstellung und ideologische Funktion indianischer Mündlichkeit in der nordamerikanischen Literatur* (Tübingen: Narr, 1991): 90.

[13] Moore, *Native Elements*, 26, 7, 250, 18.

Account of a Swiss Captain

Anonymous

The story appeared in the "Humour" section of the American Museum or Repository of Ancient and Modern Fugitive Pieces &c., Prose and Poetical, *in April 1787. Along with the* Columbian Magazine, *the* American Museum *was one of the first successful American journals. It was also one of the most long-lived in a time when many North American magazine publications folded after only a handful of issues. It was published in Philadelphia until 1792, and in its later years its publication policy changed so that it saw a significant increase in original and American stories.*

The formal features of the "Account of a Swiss Captain" are clearly anecdotal; its origins are unknown: At the time, the editor of the magazine, Matthew Carey, did not place great emphasis on the originality of the texts appearing in his magazine. Still, there are some features indicating that the story is a piece of original American fiction. At the same time, these features lift the story beyond the merely anecdotal and humorous. One such feature is the symbolic use of nationality. Another feature is the character of the American woman who, without much ado and without outside aid or advice, finds a way out of the embrace of the Swiss Captain's mercenary designs.

Account of a Swiss Captain

A certain Swiss captain of grenadiers, whose company had been cashiered, was determined, since Mars had no more employment for him, to try if he could not procure a commission in the corps of Venus; or, in other words, if he could not get a wife: and as he had no fortune of his own, he reasoned, and reasoned very justly, it was quite necessary his intended should have enough for them both.[1] The captain was one of those kind of heroes to whom the epithet of hectoring blade might readily be applied: he was near six feet high, wore a long sword, and fierce-cocked hat; add to which, he was allowed to have had the most martial pair of whiskers of any grenadier in the company to which he belonged. To curl these whiskers, to comb and twist them round his fore-finger and to admire them in the glass, formed the chief occupation and delight of his life. A man of these accomplishments, with the addition of bronze and rodomontade, of which he had a superfluity, stands at all times, and in all countries, a good chance with the ladies, as the experience of I know not how many thousand years has confirmed.

Accordingly, after a little diligent attention and artful enquiry, a young lady was found, exactly such a one as we may well suppose a person with his views would be glad to find. She was tolerably handsome, not more than three and twenty, with a good fortune; and what was the best part of the story, this fortune was entirely at her own disposal.

Our captain, who thought now or never was the time, having first found means to introduce himself as a suitor, was incessant in his endeavours to carry his cause. His tongue was eternally running in praise of her super-superlative, never-to-be-described charms; and in hyperbolical accounts of the flames, darts, and daggers, by which his lungs, liver, and midriff, were burnt up, transfixed, and gnawed away. He who, in writing a song to his sweetheart, described his heart to be without one drop of gravy, like an overdone mutton-chop, was a fool at a simile when compared to our hero.

One day, as he was ranting, kneeling, and beseeching his goddess to send him of an errand to pluck the diamond from the nose of the great mogul, and present it to her divinityship, or suffer him to step and steal the empress of China's enchanted slipper, or the queen of Sheba's cockatoo, as a small testimony of what he would undertake to prove his love; she, after a little hesitation, addressed him thus:[2]

"The protestations which you daily make, captain, as well as what you say at present, convince me there is nothing you would not do to oblige me: I therefore do not find much difficulty in telling you I am willing to be yours, if you will perform one thing which I shall request of you."

"Tell me, immaculate angel," cried our son of gunpowder: "tell me what it is; though, before you speak, be certain it is already done. Is it to find the seal of Solomon?[3] To catch the phoenix? Or draw your chariot to church with unicorns? What is the impossible act I will not undertake?"

"No, captain," replied the fair one: "I shall enjoin nothing impossible. The thing I desire, you can do with the utmost ease. It will not cost you five minutes' trouble. Yet, were it not for your so positive assurances, I should, from what I have observed, almost doubt of your compliance."

"Ah, madam!" returned he, "wrong not your slave thus; deem it impossible, that he who eats happiness, and drinks immortal life from the light of your eyes, can ever demur the thousandth part of a semi-second to execute your omnipotent behests: speak! Say! What, empress of my parched entrails, what must I perform?"

"Nay, for that matter, 'tis a mere trifle; only to cut off your whiskers, captain; that's all."

"Madam!—(Be so kind, reader, as to imagine the captain's utter astonishment) "My whiskers!—cut off my whiskers!—excuse me!—cut off my whiskers!—madam!—anything else—anything that mind can, or cannot imagine, or tongue describe—Bid me fetch you Prester John's beard, a hair at a time, and it's done. But, for my whiskers, you must grant me a salvo there."[4]

"And why so, good captain? Surely any gentleman who had but the tythe of the passion you express, would not stand upon such a trifle?"

"A trifle, madam!—my whiskers a trifle! No, madam, no—my whiskers are no trifle. Had I but a single regiment of fellows whiskered like me, I myself would be the grand Turk of Constantinople. My whiskers, madam, are the last thing I should have supposed you would have wished me to sacrifice. There is not a woman, married or single, maid, wife, or widow, that does not admire my whiskers."

"May be so, sir; but if you marry me, you must cut them off."

"And there is no other way? Must I never hope to be happy with you unless I part with my whiskers?"

"Never."

"Why then, madam, farewell: I would not part with a single hair of my whiskers if Catherine the czarina, empress of all the Russias, would make me king of the Calmucs; and so good morning to you."⁵

Had all the young ladies in like circumstances, equal penetration, they might generally rid themselves, with equal ease, of the interested and unprincipled coxcombs by whom they are pestered: they all have their whiskers; and seek for fortunes, to be able to cultivate, not cut them off.

Critical Commentary

Its obvious brevity, and its classification in the "Humour" section as well as the moral or point of the story seems to place the "Account of a Swiss Captain" in the category of the anecdote, one of the formats of short fiction that contributed to the development of the short story. While Jack B. Moore, who includes this story among his selection of early American short fictions, does not elaborate on the specifications of genre in this case, there are a number of formal elements that clearly point in the direction of the humorous anecdote: The authorial narrative situation, the limited time frame, setting, and the absence of any elaborate plot all seem to support this reading. However, there are several moments in the text that lift it beyond the merely anecdotal and humorous.

One of the aspects that reaches beyond the anecdotal is the use of nationality as symbolic space. The title of the story suggests a connection to Switzerland, but the Swiss military system is one of militia forces, which are not normally dissolved. This leads to the assumption that the "hectoring blade" is—like many Swiss in the 17th and 18th centuries, and like the Papal guards in Rome in a manner of speaking to this day—a mercenary, which creates a double sense for the story within the context of its appearance. The Captain is shown as a man who does not fight for a country, its national independence, and democracy, as so many Americans did just before the publication of the story. Instead, he will sell his fighting powers to the highest bidder—in this case the woman he intends to make his wife. The aspect of bidding is of importance; we shall take it up again later.

Also, vanity and fashion-conscious heroism are not characteristics that are commonly connected with the Swiss. Rather, earlier 18th century stereotyping would assign these qualities to the French—except that a French army had helped to defeat the British six years earlier in a war that ended colonial rule. Assigning "the most martial pair of whiskers of any grenadier" to a Swiss *miles gloriosus*, then, deflects the criticism of European efféte attitudes to another country, and it absolves the French allies from responsibility. This deflection is actually one of the most American elements of the text.

It also introduces the mercenary attitude as something worth criticizing: Not only is the officer vain and self-important, he is also trying to sell himself to a reluctant bidder, the young lady, who will in the end charge an extraordinary price for her consent. An agreement is not reached; the encounter takes on the qualities of a critique of capitalist attitudes in matters of the heart, thus going beyond the mere man vs. woman frame.

Still, within the framework of the anecdotal lies the fact that the biblical chain of motifs invoked by the whiskered Captain is extended through the allusion to the story of Samson and Delilah, the young lady in the story taking on the role of the biblical Delilah, the Captain becoming a Samson in his fear that he will loose his strength and power should his hair be cut. It also brings on a modern motif of male fears of emasculation. For the Captain, a world without a war and without his military company is a world turned upside down, especially since women have financial means at their disposal.

The female figure in the story is described as a young, rich, and clever woman. Although presented as a generic type, she shows character traits that were rather untypical for women at that time. She is pleasing enough to the eye and well-mannered, which corresponds to the expectations society had for ladies. But she is also smart, as she becomes conscious of the fact that the Captain's compliments and assertions cannot be taken seriously. Despite his exaggerated promises to undertake any impossible act he can think of in order to win her heart and convince her to marry him, the lady does not believe his claims.

This brings up a second American element: Unlike the women in Royall Tyler's *The Contrast,* a popular play that appeared the same year, the story presents a young woman who, without the outside aid or advice that would have been typical in a European conventional piece of the same period, finds a way out of the embrace of mercenary designs. The Captain's exaggerations place him squarely within the tradition of the romantic lover, a would-be Romeo promising all sorts of bounties and treasures, but all from the field of mythology or at least from antipodean extremities of the earth, and thus not of interest to the down-to-earth realist, as the young lady is described. Holding on to her own stock, and depleting the opposition's argumentation and bidding by exposing its weakness, the woman shows a shrewdness in assessing her own market value that makes her truly American.

The anecdotal point of the story is, of course, that all men have their metaphorical whiskers. However, while still following the principle of calculated brevity, the "Account of a Swiss Captain" expands the frame of the anecdote and even achieves a certain unity of effect: Everything written contributes directly to an established effect at the end of the story, though there are a variety of allusions and references along the way that bring in elements and levels of meaning that are not essential to the immediate line of argumentation, but result in a more encompassing and rounded impression. It also goes beyond the purely anecdotal in adding a somewhat obliquely stated piece of moral advice to young ladies about how to rid themselves of annoying suitors—a position that, while not revealing anything about authorial gender, at least seems to hint at female authorship, notably when comparing the message of this story to the openly chauvinistic discourse of *The Contrast* where fashion-conscious and flirtatious women are reigned in by stern and stalwart male veterans of the war. Female authorship, while impossible to prove without further evidence, is thus at least a distinct possibility for this early American (proto-) short story.

Ines Dreßler, Susanne Heiden, Alexandra Rägle

Notes

[1] This opening provides a possible chronological frame for the story: Switzerland supplied a considerable number of mercenary soldiers for the French armies in North America, for instance the Regiment de Karrer which was stationed in the Fortress of Louisbourg in Nova Scotia. After the French and Indian (or Seven Years') War, some of these units were disbanded. Not all of the soldiers returned to Europe, though. Many chose to stay in North America; our Swiss captain could be one of them.

[2] The Great Mogul was the ruler of a state in India from 1526–1858.

[3] Solomon's seal enabled him to talk to animals and demons.

[4] Prester or Presbyter John was a Christian patriarch and king. He was the main character in the widely published and, at least in Europe, well-known "Legends of Prester John."

[5] Catherine II, called Catherine the Great, was the empress of Russia from 1762–1796. This latter reference sets the timeframe of the story within the present of the contemporary reader.

Story of Julia
A Real Character
Punctilio

The sentimental story, preferably combined with some motifs of melodramatic adventure, and preferably with a happy—and morally sound—ending was arguably the most popular subgenre on the literary market in the mid to late 18th century. The "Story of Julia," which appeared in two parts in the May and June issues of The Massachusetts Magazine or Weekly Museum of Knowledge and Rational Entertainment *in 1790, can serve as an exemplary specimen in many respects. It contains most of the stock elements of a sentimental story, such as a good but soon dead father, an obedient yet soon orphaned daughter, a scheming aunt, a libertine villain, and a last-minute rescue scene. Of particular interest, however, is the fact that the story is a piece of original American fiction, which becomes apparent from the setting as well as from some of the traits of the characters. The intended realism of these features, and their deviation from the generic use of place and especially of pastoral names, also point the text in the direction of the early short story.*

Story of Julia: A Real Character

Miss *Julia Littleton*, the subject of the following narrative, was descended from reputable parents. Her mother died when she was an infant, and her father, who was the lineal descendant of a worthy race of ancestors, died when she was fifteen years old. He was possessed of an affluent fortune, which he left to *Julia*, his only child. As she was young, he committed the completion of her education to the care of her aunt, whose supposed virtue, and superiour talents, had marked her out as the most suitable person for that important trust. He was always solicitous to instil into the tender mind of *Julia*, the great worth of virtue and religion, and she had already begun to entertain an exalted opinion of the principles he inculcated. When he lay on his death bed, he called her to him, and presented to her a little book of moral and religious precepts, which he had taken great pains to collect, and bequeathed it to her as a legacy worthy of her greatest regard. "I have," said the old man, "never failed to set before you those things which I considered essential to your happiness in this world, and your salvation in the next. I am soon to quit this mortal stage, and leave you to the hazards and difficulties of this licentious state, and to the trials and shifts of precarious fortune. My conscience now acquits me of having done my duty to you as a father, and I have already the happiness to see my labours perfected in the many amiable accomplishments you possess. But I tremble, lest your youth shall betray you from the paths of virtue, and your inexperience of the evils and temptations of the world, bring on your ruin. In order that you may the more readily shun the vices and deceits of mankind, I have placed you beyond the pinching hand of penury and want. I have been able to leave you *ten thousand pounds*;[1] which, according to my directions, will be lodged in the hands of Mrs. *Sumpter*, your aunt; the interest of which you are to have annually for your support; and when you arrive at the age of eighteen, you are to have the principle to dispose of as you think best. To you I recommend her as a faithful mistress, and a sincere friend. She is well calculated to give you instruction; and if you obey her dictates, you will be happy. I die in peace; assuring myself that you will shun the evils which surround you; pay the most sacred regard to the duties of religion; obey the dictates of virtue and not forget to open and peruse your little book. Finally, I commit you into the hands of God!"

As soon as *Littleton* had ended his lesson, he clasped his daughter by the hand, and then closed his eyes in death. It may be readily supposed, that this last and trying scene made a powerful impression upon the mind of *Julia*, who was naturally prone to pay the greatest reverence to the injunctions of her father; and ever put the most implicit confidence in his paternal concern for her happiness. The thoughts of being left destitute of a parent to protect her, and no friend in whom she could confide, save an aunt, who, she supposed, could not be over interested in her welfare; were considerations sufficient to load her with insupportable grief. A thousand fearful apprehensions of one day incurring her aunt's displeasure, and then being exposed to the attacks of seeming, but unprincipled friends; her liableness to error; and also her fond predilection for study, and the performance of the Christian duties; now apt they were to incur the censure and envy of the greatest part of mankind. All these she viewed as so many indications of her ruin; and they constantly appeared to her perturbed senses, as so many frightful pictures of her destruction. A deep melancholy preyed upon her constitution, and enfeebled her frame. But her natal fortitude finally surmounted these gloomy spectres, and enabled her to assume a more elevated air. Her sprightly vivacity gradually returned; her hopes revived, and prospects brightened. She still remained in her father's house, under the care of the house keeper; but soon began to turn her attention towards her aunt, who resided in New York. In order to acquaint her of her duty she owed her, and of her intention to fulfil the incumbent obligations, she wrote her the following letter:

"Dear Aunt,

"Nothing can pain me more than that I am obliged to communicate to you the sudden death of an indulgent father. I should have performed that task before now, but I trust the pressure of woes, with which I am loaded, will sufficiently apologize for the delay. The last solemn scene I had to endure, is not as yet erased from my mind, so that I can only observe, that before he bid adieu to things below, he recommended me to your care and protection; and has left you the sole guardian of my happiness and fortune. I hope in all things to merit your regard, and shall strive to render myself deserving of your kind patronage and protection. Any commands you may wish to communicate relative to my removal, or otherwise, shall be faithfully observed by your much afflicted niece."

In the mean time *Julia* endeavoured to reconcile her mind to the berieving stroke of providence, and be prepared to encounter every calamity to which she might be exposed. She did not fail to consult her little book of precepts, and drew from thence a store of useful knowledge. It contained rules for her future conduct in life; and was embellished with all the beauties necessary to charm and captivate a young and delicate mind. But these, separately considered, did not make the greatest impression: the book itself was the dying legacy of a father, whose memory she was determined to perpetuate by a faithful adherence to his friendly and paternal admonitions. This she considered as her most durable treasure; and was willing to sacrifice every personal consideration to attain its real excellencies. With this view, the time that was not necessarily taken up in the management of her domestic concerns, she devoted to the pursuits of learning; and the acquisition of those noble endowments, which throw a lustre on the female character. She was happily calculated for this employment. Her mind was naturally strong, and highly ornamented with the richest delicacies of nature, as well as improved art, and capable of making great proficiency in her studies. Her judgment was clear, her penetration remarkably great, and memory tenacious: all these conspired, in an eminent degree, to give her the advantage over many others; and she improved it to the admiration of the more learned and sagacious.

At the end of three months *Julia* received a lengthy letter from her aunt, part of which is extracted for the reader to peruse.

"My dear Julia,

"I should have answered your's before this, but the heavy tidings of my brother's death so much oppressed me, that I found it to difficult to survive their first shock. I sincerely lament your loss, and will do every thing in my power to render your future life happy; and wipe the tear of affliction from the eye of innocence. Since your kind father has been so good as to appoint me the sole guardian of your life and property, nothing shall be wanting on my part to render myself deserving of his confidence, and merit your approbation. This stroke of mortality ought to be improved by you as a lesson of instruction; and put you upon *remembering your creator in the days of your youth.*[2] Let not the desponding cares, with which you are surrounded, disturb your quiet, nor indulge an excessive mourning; but bring yourself to acquiesce in the awful dispensation, and say, *the will of the Lord be done.*[3] Persons of your age and condition are too apt to feed upon their own melancholy, and encourage the stream of agonizing woe, till it becomes impossible to impede its impetuous torrent. Therefore absorb your grief; resolve to erase the impression of distress and anguish from your mind, and assume a lively temper. This will be conducive to your health and happiness; and be a mean of preserving your life, and increasing your usefulness in the world.

"But I would not have you blot out the memory of a departed friend. Let the good advice and instruction of him, who has made his exit to better climes, sink deep in your mind. You are now set afloat amid the dangers of a boisterous ocean, whose swelling billows may one day drive your frail bark upon the precarious shores of adversity. Some unforeseen event may wound your peace, and blacken your reputation. We are all subject to the vicissitudes of capricious fortune; she heaps her favours upon some; to others she proves unkind. Be prepared to withstand the attacks of calumny; ward off the poisoned arrows of envy; and disappoint the intrigues of ambition. These can only be effected by the practice of virtue and piety; the only permanent basis on which we can found our happiness. As age comes on, your knowledge of the world will increase, which will lead you to entertain more enlarged views of the excellency of those precepts, that have often been inculcated for your good, and I hope not without effect. The vanities and allurements of this life will diminish, and the noble and sublime refinement of a virtuous education, swell your bosom with a just abhorrence of vice and wickedness.

"I wish you to remain for a while in your present situation. In the mean time I will prepare for your reception; and when that is done, you shall hear again from your affectionate aunt."

It is impossible to describe the painful emotions which this letter occasioned. On the one hand *Julia* found herself much disappointed in not setting out immediately to New York: on the other, the want of a relative in whom she could securely confide; the uncertain destiny of herself and fortune in the midst of a licentious world, and hourly exposed to the impositions of perfidious and unprincipled beings, did not a little contribute to her uneasiness. In this hour of extreme difficulty, when restless anxiety had severely shocked her frame, she had recourse to her little book of precepts. She happened to turn to a chapter, which treated of the diseases of the mind, and the antidote there prescribed was drawn from scripture, *whatever be thy condition, be thou therewith content.*[4] This salutary counsel suddenly engrossed her attention, and scattered the gathering storms of apprehension from her mind. Her conscious rectitude *made her soar above the vanities of the world*,[5] and enabled her to partake of those solid enjoyments which flow a heart, free from pride, *pure without alloy.*[6]

After the death of her papa, she refused, for some time, to see any company, except what was necessary to the execution of her daily concerns. This recluse way of living was incompatible with the lively dictates of her mind; far from being agreeable to her natural disposition; and not a little prejudicial to her health. She was always considered as being possessed of a much gayer turn than most ladies of her age; but she had judgment enough to distinguish real merit. She resolved to entertain some few friends, and chose those for her most intimate connections, whose virtue and piety, marked them out as the most proper objects of her esteem and imitation. With these she conversed at times, and received no little advantage from their friendly instructions. She began to delight herself in social intercourse, and became an object of love and respect in the gayer circles of the town. But she would not suffer these so far to attract her attention as to divert her mind from her peculiar situation, or make her neglect her studies, and other useful amusements. She became convinced, that a little company tended to make her more easy and happy. It served, in some degree, to dissipate her former troubles, and obscured the gloomy spectres, and visionary predictions, with which her imagination was crowded.

But this tranquil state was of short duration. Three months had now elapsed, and no news from her aunt. Her patience was put to the test. Her anxiety to get to New York rose in proportion as the time was prolonged, and she now began to mention her disappointment with tears of regret. Her thoughts were so much bent upon this journey, that her friends were apprehensive of some fatal disorder; and therefore concluded to persuade her to take the country air. They were intimate with the *B—* family, of D—, to whom they strongly recommended the unfortunate *Julia*. Miss *Harriot B—*, by the permission of her parents, dispatched a servant with a very polite billet to *Julia*, asking the pleasure of her acquaintance, and requesting her to spend a month with her in the country.

Story of Julia

Julia met with no difficulty in obtaining the consent of her friends. She accepted the invitation, and retired to D—, leaving the management of her affairs to her domestics. Here, in this romantic vale which exhibited every thing necessary to please the fancy and gratify the sight, she constantly attended to the duties of religion, and in the acquisition of those moral precepts, which shined forth with distinguished lustre in the more advanced period of her life.

At last the welcome message arrived with instructions for *Julia* to repair to New York. However much animated in obeying this summons; yet she was secretly convinced that her aunt had behaved very coolly towards her, and had almost been guilty of a breach of friendship in not sending for her sooner. But this consideration did not retard her progress. The next day she took leave of her friends; and the day after pursued on her journey. She took along with her a maid; besides two other servants, with whom she entrusted her money, and other articles; all of which she delivered into the possession of her aunt.

Here begins the era of the misfortunes, to which the ill fated *Julia* was exposed. The seemingly affectionate reception she experienced, served to abate her fears respecting the unfriendly disposition of her aunt, and for a while kept her in the pleasing delusion. But an event soon happened that disclosed the views of the treacherous aunt, which shall soon be related. For the present, we will make a few introductory observations, which may tend to elucidate the subsequent narrative.

Mrs. *Sumpter* had always flattered herself that *Littleton* would bestow upon her no small part of his fortune, as he had only one lineal heir; whose circumstances would not require more than one half of it. This she early communicated to some intimate friends, and would undoubtedly have done it to her brother himself, had not his death prevented. Perhaps he considered that the affluent circumstances of his sister did not need his assistance. But he amply provided for the education and expenses of *Julia*, by granting to his sister the income of certain parts of his real estate during her natural life, and then to revert to his daughter. Being this frustrated, she at once determined to obtain by fraud and perfidy, what she could not legally possess. The contrivance of this scheme retarded *Julia's* journey to New York: for the deceitful aunt was anxious to have her plots ripe for execution before she arrived, so that she might the more readily avoid suspicion; and secretly work out the ruin of the unsuspecting innocent.

Second Part

Now comes the event which was just mentioned. The artful and intriguing aunt had agreed to betray the harmless *Julia* into the hands of Captain Piemont, whose libertine principles were well known, and who was then bound on a voyage to the Cape of Good Hope. But to accomplish it so as to clear herself of suspicion, was still more difficult. The thoughts of so valuable an acquisition, fired the bosom of the insidious Piemont with the most brutal desires. He resolved to sacrifice his interest, his honour, and even his life, to complete the conquest. He was soon introduced to *Julia* as a gentleman of a good character, and highly recommended by the aunt as a person with whom she might safely cultivate an intimate friendship, and at the same time expressed a wish that they might establish a still closer connection. This untimely insinuation carried with it the appearance of a sanguinary disposition, rather than exhibited the least degree of love and caution. Piemont, it is true, was possessed of many exterior accomplishments, which could not fail of making some impression upon a mind, naturally susceptible of the softer feelings of humanity; but she had discernment enough to pry into the understanding of his heart, the religion he possessed, his moral conduct in life, and well knew how to distinguish real affection from pretended friendship. She was fully convinced that his addresses were founded upon the prospects of wealth, for it seems he did not fully understand the motives of Mrs. *Sumpter*, in forwarding his purposes; neither did *Julia* in the least suspect that he had in contemplation the ruin of her character, and the staining of her virtue. By whatever motives he might at first be actuated, the charms and accomplishments of the destined victim to his licentious views, soon began to soften his heart, and fill his bosom with quite different feelings. He would have willingly made her the most honourable proposals, but the fear of disappointment prevented him; and his predominant passion suggesting the vilest deceit, he became rigorously bent upon the enjoyment of the last favour, not by artful flattery, because he was convinced that such a measure would never melt her into kindness; but by treachery and violence, the last resort of the wicked.

Many plans were laid, and schemes concerted to accomplish these diabolic purposes; but the prudence rather than the suspicions of *Julia*, eluded their efforts. She was resolved to trust no friend, much more to expose herself to the attacks of those, whose conduct had rendered them not only odious, but dangerous; and the uncommon reserve with which her aunt treated her, was sufficient to make her confidence doubtful. With this resolution, she was determined to meet the frowns of fortune; and her own conscious innocence served to keep her bosom serene and calm, and *left not a sting behind.*[7]

But the crafty foes of her happiness persevered in their designs, and finally deceived the afflicted *Julia*. She had contracted an intimate acquaintance with the amiable Miss *Sophia Bayard*. This was noticed by Piemont, and Mrs. *Sumpter*. They resolved to make use of her name, in order to accomplish their wishes. They forged a billet in *Sophia's* name, directed to *Julia*, requesting the pleasure of her company the ensuing evening to drink tea on board Piemont's ship, as he had very politely given her an invitation, and the privilege of choosing what party she pleased to accompany her, and that she would meet her on *M'Dougal's* pier, (so called) from which place they were to take boat, precisely at six o'clock. *Julia* was not a little perplexed in her mind, for she was always solicitous to avoid doing any thing which might look like suspicion, and ever paid the greatest seeming deference to the advice of her aunt; and affected to place implicit confidence in the virtue of those, to whom she was recommended. In order still to preserve the appearance of unsuspicion, she accepted the invitation. When she arrived at the pier she found a boat ready for her reception, and on inquiring after *Sophia*, was informed that she had gone on board, but had left her compliments and desired her to proceed after her. She did not hesitate to comply. But when she entered the ship, how great was her astonishment! She searched for *Sophia*—Alas! Nobody was to be seen but Piemont. He was confused, and knew not what to say, but at last he made out to utter—*Come, amiable* Julia, *and make yourself contented, I will endeavour to make your situation agreeable; the company have not arrived.* She stood speechless, but knowing her situation to be perilous, was resolved to assume a boldness proportionable to her danger. "What! cried she hastily, have you the wickedness to seek the ruin of an unhappy female? Have I done any thing to merit such treatment? Or rather have I not always treated you with friendship and respect? O, can you be so cruel as to ruin one, who never did you any hurt! What feelings must you have to betray me from the protection of the world, and then to meditate the violence I so justly apprehend! For God's sake, if you have any compassion; if you can melt at other's woes; if you are possessed of one generous sentiment; if distress; if misfortunes can move your feelings, pray have pity on me! I am in your hands, satiate your brutal desires, and then abandon me to infamy and despair! My life is of no value; I had much rather sacrifice it than to lose my honour! Here! (opening her bosom) here plunge in your dagger, and relieve my misery! Good God! thou knowest the purity of my heart! Protect me; and forgive thou the offender!"

The distress and anguish pictured in the countenance of *Julia*; the severe, though just reprimand she had given, and the most fervent ejaculations, for a moment softened the heart of Piemont, and caused tears to flow.

Now it happened, that the mate of the ship was a native to Boston, had obtained a liberal education—had acquired many accomplishments—had made great proficiency in his classical studies, and had also been so fortunate as to establish a shining reputation; but poverty compelled him to renounce the more active and conspicuous scenes of life, and seek a livelihood upon the ocean. He had been intimately acquainted with *Littleton*; had experienced many of his favours, and was no stranger to the virtues of *Julia*; but his absence had erased him from her mind, and whether he was dead or alive, she did not know. This knowledge and acquaintance, he carefully concealed from Piemont, who was continually boasting of his libertine adventures, and how he intended to triumph over the virtue of the beautiful *Julia*.

Edwards (for that was the mate's name) was not in a situation to apprize her of her danger. He reflected with painful anxiety upon the resolute designs of Piemont, but he was resolved to defeat them, and save the harmless fair from destruction. The natural goodness of his heart led him to espouse the cause of innocence, and save the unfortunate *Julia* from impending ruin, at the risk of his own life and reputation. He was no stranger to the intended attempt of Piemont to decoy her on board, and then to accomplish his wishes. For the purpose of defeating his intentions, *Edwards* went to the door of the cabin, and through the key hole observed all that passed, was well armed, and prepared to enter as soon as necessity required.

In the mean time *Julia* pursued her intreaties, and went so far as to conjure Piemont by every tie of friendship and humanity, by the sacred laws of honour, and the dreadful wrath of offended heaven, to set her on shore—but her expostulations were unavailing. "How can you, said she, be a witness to my disgrace, and not be covered with shame! How can you bear to make me become an outcast, and forfeit my title to virtue, and be forever excluded from entering the pure abodes of the righteous." Be pleased to show some pity towards my unhappy condition, and not forget the day when you must account for this unexampled treachery! I did not think you could be so cruel." Although he had not made any forcible attempt upon her virtue, yet his intentions were obvious, by betraying her on board in a clandestine manner, and under the specious pretence of a friendly visit; and the whole scene conducted by deception too, which must shock the ear of delicacy. As soon as she concluded her last sentence, she melted into tears, and dropped back into her chair. Piemont pretended great humanity—drew near her—pressed her hand, and feigned to water it with his tears. He made use of every art to persuade her to a compliance, alledging, that she was in his power, that as he was guilty of seducing her, he would make her ample amends by tendering her his hand in a way which she deemed the most honourable. But finding his arguments fail, and suddenly agitated at the repulse, he began to proceed to extremities. She entreated his pity, and struggled hard. At this critical moment, *Edwards* dashed open the door, and flew to her relief. They were all equally astonished. Piemont little expected an assault. *Edwards*'s situation was not a little disagreeable, for he had ventured to intrude himself by force into the presence of his superior officer, and defeated his flattering prospects. Nothing can describe the feelings of *Julia*. At first she suspected he was an accomplice in Piemont's intended wickedness, but his countenance, in which she read the intentions of his heart, soon convinced her that he was her deliverer; and on a sudden, recollecting his features, flew into his arms in the most eager transports. This quick transition from deep despair to the most unspeakable joy, quite overpowered the disconsolate *Julia*, and she fell into a swoon. During this time, Piemont viewed what had happened with the utmost trepidation and amazement; not daring to oppose. As soon as *Julia* recovered, *Edwards* conducted her on shore, leaving poor Piemont behind them, mortified and confounded at the novel scene that had been exhibited. So great was his disappointment, and the reflection of his having lost the esteem of the good and virtuous, without completing his anticipated sacrifice, that he spent the night in hopeless despair of ever retrieving his reputation. Sometimes he thought of writing to *Julia*, and in the most pathetic language to crave her pardon and solicit her friendship. But his guilt was so enormous, as convinced him that such a measure would have no effect. This he well knew, and thus his mind was perpetually vibrating between inclination and the certainty of proving unsuccessful in his attempts of reconciliation; till at length reflection wasted his frame, and impaired his constitution. He forever after secluded himself from society, and lived like an outcast and one who had forfeited all claim to the notice of civilized men; and like one, too, who was conscious that his conduct was such as precluded him from the enjoyments of this life, and the happiness of that which is to come.

It is now time to draw the curtain of oblivion over the tragic scene, and employ our thoughts upon a more pleasing subject.

The combination of circumstances which had hitherto tended to render the conduct of Mrs. *Sumpter* strongly suspected, were now become apparent, and her participation in Piemont's villany no longer doubted; *Julia* thought it prudent to avoid her, and went immediately to the apartment of Miss *Sophia Bayard*, to whom she related every circumstance relative to her dangerous excursion; the fearful apprehension of returning to her aunt, and was soon led to discover the deception of the billet. Miss Bayard relieved her from her anxiety by wishing her to make herself easy in her present situation.

The next day she wrote to her aunt a particular account of what had happened, alledging, by way of excuse, that she was suddenly taken ill, which was the cause of her absence the preceding evening; but received for answer, *that she must come directly.* This positive command not a little perplexed her. On the one hand she considered, that, if obeyed, she was liable to still greater impositions, and those, too, which would end in the completion of her ruin; for she plainly saw that one disappointment only prepared the way for some more fatal experiment: on the other, she was convinced, that if she refused to comply with her aunt's injunctions, her fortune would be exposed, and no doubt the avaricious desires of pretended friends would swallow it up, and leave her destitute and dependent. She carefully weighed all these circumstances, and came to the resolution of sacrificing every consideration of interest to her personal safety. The reflection, however, of becoming dependent and forlorn, did not, at first, so much shock her feelings; for the series of misfortunes to which she had been exposed, rendered her mind less susceptible of impression. But reflection, and the rugged scenes which opened to her view, cast a gloomy shade over her mind, and for a while disturbed her tranquil repose.

From this period, *Edwards* became solicitous for the happiness of *Julia*, and poverty alone prevented him from openly avowing his passion. She, on her part, equally esteemed him for his good disposition, integrity and virtue, and felt herself under no final obligation to him for her late deliverance from impending ruin. Their mutual harmony and love daily increased, till, at last, *Edwards*, seeing no prospect of being in a situation to offer her his hand, and her own interest being as yet precarious, took his leave, and sailed for Canton, in China, in hopes that fortune would so far smile upon him, as to return him in better circumstances, and enable him to complete his connexion with *Julia*. Although their intimacy was great, yet they were both very cautious in opening their sentiments, both fearful of not meeting a favourable reception, which would not a little mortify the one who first made the proposition. When they parted, the tears shed were sure testimonies of the tender passion of both, and they were no longer in doubt as to the sincerity of each other's intentions. Notwithstanding she affected to maintain her usual vivacity, yet she appeared evidently dejected, and the cause of it was easily explained. She applied herself to reading and seemed to relish retirement. She would spend hours in walking in the garden in a very pensive mood. She had contracted such a state for reading *The Vicar of Wakefield*,[8] that she never amused herself more agreeably, and the mournful progress of the good old man, and his amiable family, through life, would draw tears from her eyes. She greatly admired the ballad of the two lovers, who had fled from society, and met in the lonely wilderness, as typical of her own situation.[9] The striking simplicity of the style and sentiment, were captivating; and whilst secluded from the busy scenes of life, and wandering amid the shady bowers, she has been often heard to repeat the lines:—

> Forlorn and lost I tread,
> With fainting steps and slow![10]

These were the mournful accents of the distressed female, addressed to her unknown lover; and were never more applicable than to *Julia*, when separated from the only object of her affections.

An event soon happened, which determined the fate of *Julia's* fortune. Her aunt very unjustly cast her off as unworthy of her regard, and debarred her from having any part or lot in the inheritance of her father. This could not be prevented, as *Littleton* placed such implicit confidence in the rectitude of his sister, that he little thought of guarding his property against any encroachments. However severe this stroke would have been to the generality of mankind, it did not seem to add to the perturbed feelings of *Julia*, for her misfortunes before had arisen to as great a height as she was capable of enduring, and she bore this last painful stroke with Christian fortitude and philosophy. The family in which she had resided since she left her aunt, were very kind, and gave her to understand, that she was henceforth to be considered as a daughter.

The amusements of the world now became insipid; nevertheless she acted her part with such a grace, that it required the greatest penetration to discover her afflictions. She never complained, but praised her maker, that she had been hitherto preserved. She constantly attended to the duties of religion, for she rightly considered, that every other concern of life depended on these, without which her best services would prove unacceptable in the sight of her creator. She happily divided her time between these duties and other rational amusements, so as not to injure her health by too great application to one constant employment. In this way she spent nearly two years without hearing from *Edwards*, about whose fate she began to entertain some fearful apprehensions. But the great rewarder of good, and punisher of evil, never suffers the virtuous to perish. At last the long wished for *Edwards* arrived. He flew to inquire the fate of *Julia*. Both were agreeably delighted. Their first meeting was attended with mutual pleasure. Fortune had so far dealt out her favours, as to return him in health and in the possession of a competency of wealth. Their affection for each other was great. He made proposals of marriage, which met the approbation of *Julia*. They were accordingly united in the bands of Hymen; and if Love and Virtue can render this life agreeable, *Edwards* and *Julia* must be happy.

Critical Commentary

In "Story of Julia" the names individualize the characters—at least at first sight this is one of the most modern and American features of the text. Upon closer inspection, however, the names as well as the rest of the text still show signs of the generic and typical, though cleverly camouflaged: Julia means "youthful" and "downy-haired"; Piemont's Franco-Italian name alone was enough to signal to the experienced reader the advent of the libertine villain; and Edwards' Anglo-Saxon name, fittingly enough, means "prosperous guardian."

Sentimental fiction in *The Massachusetts Magazine* as well as elsewhere served a crucial purpose in the late 18th century: it demarcated the border between acceptable and unacceptable behavior. This intention is underlined by the author's pen name "Punctilio," a direct reference to etiquette and appropriate behavior. Sentimental fiction went beyond the older conduct books, however, in fictionalizing its moral advice around perils and temptations faced by young females.

> For the young female reader, the sentimental novel, probably for the first time in literary history, put her own fantasy life at the center of the literary text and thus acknowledged her as a potential heroine.[11]

The genre is originally British. It began its course as an offshoot of the conduct and courtesy books of the early 18th century, with Samuel Richardson's *Pamela or Virtue Rewarded* setting the pace and tone for all those to follow after its publication in 1740. Considered "a new species of writing designed to turn young people into a course of reading different from the pomp and parade of romance-writing,"[12] *Pamela* became a bestseller at home as well as in the colonies. In British North America, it was reprinted by none other than Benjamin Franklin in 1744. Other novels and stories followed, the popularity of Richardson of course leading to numerous attempts at copying his formula on both sides of the Atlantic. But whereas Jack B. Moore described "The Story of Constantius and Pulchera," which appeared in the *Gentleman and Lady's Town and Country Magazine* in 1789/90, as "an almost classic example of a story sentimental in pattern and outline, but based more or less on some facts and probabilities of the American experience" the present story goes beyond Moore's example in trying to establish a believable American context.[13]

The standard format of sentimental fictions is clearly formulaic: An innocent yet gullible young woman has lost, or loses early in the tale, her mother, or father, or both, and is either without further help, chaperone, or guardian, or that guardian proves untrustworthy, or helpless against the powers of a male seducer. The seducer manages to persuade or overpower his female victim, and he either elopes with her or she is ostracized by society. Afterward, the seducer always abandons the woman—either out of sheer malevolence, or irresponsibility, sometimes because he is killed by her father, or brother, or somebody else. The young woman usually perishes and dies, often in childbirth.

Even a superficial comparison between this formula and the story at hand already unveils a number of deviations and dissimilarities. The first, and a recognizably American element, is the fact that the girl does not even consider falling for available temptations. She holds fast to the teachings of her father, the backbone of which are instructions from the Bible. Against this combination of fatherly and godly protection, the machinations of the evil aunt and her minion cannot prevail—a strongly Puritan motif quite fittingly employed in a Boston-based publication.

With no chance of seducing Julia, the scheming aunt and the libertine captain resort to violence. This is where the text leaves the beaten track of conventional sentimental fiction to incorporate plot elements and motifs from the melodrama. Based on a similar configuration, and personalizing good and evil in even more binary oppositional constructions, the melodrama adds intrigue, violence, and even moderate instances of pornography—there is a back-and-forth of determination in Piemont, and consequently a sequence of tearful withdrawal and direct assault; plus, Julia actually bares her bosom, and there is a male-female embrace, though with the hero and deliverer, which can be seen as a substitute for the prevented rape of the heroine.

The hero, in turn, is designed so as to leave no doubt about his moral as well as economic qualities and qualifications: Edwards transgresses the borders of good conduct in threatening his superior officer—though he does not actually attack him physically, which would apparently have been unacceptable. He also comes into physical contact with the heroine in a melodramatic fashion, but there is no insinuation that this might result in a scenario reminiscent of Heinrich v. Kleist's ironic reversal of the melodramatic rescue in *The Marquise of O.* Instead, Edwards, much like the knight errand of the mediaeval romance, has to steer clear of his beloved for two years to prove himself worthy; a worthiness expressed not in heroic deeds but, in true New England Calvinist fashion, through the collection of an economic fortune in overseas trade. Simultaneously, the heroine is chastened and reduced to desexualized and frugal behavior again in keeping with New England Calvinist ideals.

The admixture of the sentimental and the melodramatic provides for a rather curious integration of religious doctrine and sensational action, of moral and proper conduct and titillating sensuality. As a textual strategy, the use of ambiguity and ambivalence is a familiar feature of the short story in its more developed form; its antecedents are clearly visible here.

Not that readers were told to think of the "Story of Julia" as fiction. The subtitle "A Real Character" was probably meant to convey to readers at least a sense of verisimilitude, enhanced by the fact that other than in the above mentioned "Story of Constantius and Pulchera" the names of Piemont and Edwards, Julia Littleton and Mrs. Sumpter, though loaded with additional connotations, are everyday names. The same holds true for the American features of the setting. New York exists, yet it also signifies beyond its qualities as a North American seaport. The clearly oppositional relation between the safe and protected countryside and the dangerous city is a common feature of romantic as well as sentimental fiction; the fact that for the "Story of Julia" New York is chosen to embody the center of cosmopolitan entertainment, and with that of the moral as well as physical dangers of civilization, is something that has accompanied American literature ever since. These same features also move the story in the direction of the early short story with its clearly more realist approach.

The sea represents the most ambivalent space. As in other stories ("The Story of the Captain's Wife and an Aged Woman" in this collection) it seems to bring out the best and the worst in men, producing a Piemont as well as an Edwards, who "had, like many another educated New Englander . . . gone to sea to seek his fortune." This feature, however, is not particular to American letters, but even more commonly identified with the English seafaring novel.

With *Punctilio* not identified (though, given the male form of the Medieval Latin noun *punctilius* similar in meaning to the English *punctilio*, most likely a male writer), and considering the unreliability of American figures and settings actively denoting American origin in the short fiction of the period, the "Story of Julia" might still have been of European origin, with place names and some traits of character altered. This apparently happened in some cases, but the presence of Calvinist or Puritan sentiment and motifs seems to be rather deeply ingrained in Julia's story, and the direction of these motifs together with the other elements of the text toward a calculated effect are too obvious to be accidental. Published in the same issues of the magazine that also contained essays on a "Theory of Moral Sentiments" and a "Disquisition upon the Theology and Morals of the New Testament," the moral and didactic intent appear unquestionable.

Admittedly, the "Story of Julia" provided a reading experience more loaded with action and titillating suspense than might be expected at first, considering the essays surrounding it. However, *The Massachusetts Magazine* was apparently aiming at a more general readership, some of which were looking for information, or for counsel and advice. Others were simply looking for entertainment.

With its variety of motifs and potential meanings, the "Story of Julia" served different audiences simultaneously, an aspect that makes it a predecessor of the modern short story.

Vanessa Kern, Stefanie Kauntz

Notes

[1] This roughly equals $750,000 today.

[2] Ecclesiastes 12:1.

[3] Acts 21:14.

[4] Philippians 4:11: "Not that I speak in respect of want: for I have learned, in whatsoever state I am, therewith to be content."

[5] This is not a verbatim citation but might refer to Proverbs 30:8: "Remove far from me vanity and lies: give me neither poverty nor riches; feed me with food convenient for me." This seems to fit the further development of the story.

[6] Probably a reference to James 3:17: "But the wisdom that is from above is first pure, then peaceable, gentle, and easy to be intreated, full of mercy and good fruits, without partiality, and without hypocrisy." Both passages together could also be a reference to Psalm 24:4: "He that hath clean hands, and a pure heart; who hath not lifted up his soul into vanity, nor sworn deceitfully."

[7] Even though this passage is emphasized the same way biblical references are throughout the text, this one seems to refer to a proverb: "The sting of a reproach is in the truth of it."

[8] A sentimental novel by Oliver Goldsmith, published in 1766.

[9] The "Ballad" mentioned in the *Story of Julia* tells the story of two lovers of different social status being reunited after the poor suitor's assumed suicide. The ballad is delivered by the character of the (assumedly) poor Mr. Burchell, who earlier saved the

character Sophia from drowning. Not unlike the story at hand, the two are attracted to each other after this incident.

[10] Goldsmith, 39.

[11] Winfried Fluck, "Novels of Transition: From Sentimental Novel to Domestic Novel," *The Construction and Contestation of American Culture and Identities in the Early National Period*, ed. Udo Hebel (Heidelberg: Winter, 1999): 98.

[12] Herbert Ross Brown, *The Sentimental Novel in America 1789–1860* (New York: Pageant, 1956): 28.

[13] Jack B. Moore, *Native Elements in American Magazine Short Fiction: 1741–1800*, diss. U of North Carolina, 1963: 114.

Fidele: Or the Faithful Shepherd
An American Tale Founded on Literal Truth
Caloc

This story was first published in May 1791 in The Massachusetts Magazine *(1789–1796). With* The New-York Magazine, *it was the longest-lived U. S. magazine in the 18th century. Editor Isaiah Thomas encouraged his readership to contribute original literary works and essays. The following story is probably such an original American text. Its characters and sentiments mirror established Anglo-European models, but the story also features some references to contemporary political events, as well as Republican thought.*

The author of "Fidele," semi-identified as "J. L. Caloc, a son of Apollo," in the December 1793 issue, ranks among the more frequent contributors to the magazine. Caloc's ode "The Consolation" in the February 1790 issue is dedicated to "Constantia." This is of particular interest since it hints at the existence of a network of authors: "Constantia" was the first nom de plume used by Sarah Wentworth Morton (1759–1846), the prominent New England writer and supporter of independence and abolitionism. Caloc's style, however, is considerably inferior to Morton's.

Fidele: Or the Faithful Shepherd
An American Tale Founded on Literal Truth

The subject of the present historiette, was the only child of a once respectable mechanic, in a neighbouring state, whose natural genius, assisted by intense application, had removed him from the humble grade, to the more exalted sphere of a practitioner at law. Uprightness, integrity, and inflexible honesty, which marked his character in the valley of obscurity, "grew with his growth, and strengthened with his strength," as he ascended in the scale of public reputation. His practice was confessedly extensive; but his gains inconsiderable, as the causes of the oppressed poor were dear to his soul, without expectance of fee, or hope of reward.

 The protection of great villains, he invariably left to the protection of still greater; nor ever prostituted his talents to subserve the opulent rogue. The nature of Horatio's profession afforded vast opportunities of investigating the springs of human action. He accurately noticed the rise, progress and termination of those discordant passions, which wind through the labyrinth of legal disputes; and determined that Fidele should be educated without the pale of wordy war; only imbuing his mind with some general theoretical definitions, sufficient to render him a judge of right and wrong; or assist a neighbour as the peaceful arbitrator of rural differences. Eighteen vernal suns had already revolved; the nineteenth began to smile on Fidele, when his father was suddenly arrested by the angel of malignant fever, and hastened to that prison bourne from whence no captive returns. "My son, my only child (said the affectionate father, as he clasped the trembling hand of Fidele) lessons of wisdom, matured by the experience of seventy summers, the pencil of tender solicitude, has engraven on thy bosom. I trust, and the hope is pleasing in death, that no other power, but the corroding energy of time, can erase the precepts of paternal love. Remember, my boy, the small inheritance that I leave to your charge, is a sacred fiduciary deposit. It was acquired by the toils of honest industry, labouring in the cause of unprotected innocence. I have heard the bursting carol of the widow's grateful heart salute me, amid these peaceful walks, as the guardian friend of helpless virtue. I have seen the opening furrows of my little field, watered by those silent tears of gratitude that flowed from the eye of the fatherless. My son, reverence the bones of thy father when hearsed in the channel. Commit all that is mortal to the tomb hewn out of the rock, where the dust of thy mother reposes in everlasting quiet. Prefer this humble mansion, it is unpolluted with a guilty sigh, to the magnificent palace of unrighteous gain. In the warm fervor of faith, nothing doubting, I have commended thy best interests in time, and the still more glorious that await thee in futurity, to the fountain of ineffable benedictions. In the visions of the night, that approximates fast to the day spring of felicity, I have received an answer of peace. A religious observance of probity in all the commerce of life, the heaven wrought shield; is thine. One caution yet remains, it presses on this beating heart. Insensibility to the charms of the virtuous fair, possesses a degree of cool criminality. At a proper age, may prudence direct thy choice, to some village maiden, rich in innocence alone. With her, thy moments shall glide away smooth, as the placid river, whose waters steal silent to the ocean. Thy father's spirit shall witness the connubial scene; and bless you as he passes by. Adieu, my darling boy; the god of thy fathers be the portion of Fidele."

A gentle sigh emancipated the good man's soul—the smile of brighter worlds serenely sat on his faltering tongue. Fidele faithfully mourned the best of earthly parents. For several months he gave himself up to the luxury of woe. Respected by his seniors, beloved of his fellows, the admiration of the blooming fair, he arose in the morn of manhood, tall as the cedar of the upland forest, graceful as the hind of the vernal moons, more beautiful than the genius of spring, and innocent as the white pinioned dove. The elegant Zephyra abode not far from the place of his dwelling. Her form was majestic as the fabled goddess of the woods. Her mind accomplished as *Philenia's*, the daughter of the skies.[1] She was selected as the partner of Fidele, at a rural fete; he viewed her with a delicate yet impassioned regard: She looked upon the engaging youth with reciprocal tenderness. The melting language of the ever speaking eye revealed their mutual fondness. Fidele would have been happy in more direct advances; but his circumstances forbade a probable increase of expense. In these trying situations of two amiable hearts, formed by similarity of sentiment to render each other blest, there is a *je ne sais quoy* peculiarly interesting, exquisitely affecting. Every votary of the humanizing sensations, must spontaneously wish to relieve both from their tender embarrassment; and to render these deserving timid lovers, as openly happy, as they were sentimentally attached. At this moment of indecision on the one part, of fluctuating hope on the other, a truly dignified character presented himself in the capital upon a benevolent visit to his "friends and fellow citizens." The hoary sire leaned worshipping upon his staff, as he blest his closing eyes. The young man and maiden viewed the deliverer of America, "the soul of peace, the conquering arm of war," with almost religious veneration.[2] Amid those numbers, which the distant hamlet poured forth on the populous town, Fidele swelled the train of the good, the therefore great. Almira, the only daughter of an eminent India merchant, distinguished the faithful shepherd, as her brilliant eyes roved among the crowd. He seemed to her wondering view, a star let drop from brighter spheres to grace the rapturous scene. She was irresistibly, fatally smitten with his person; and enjoining a confidential female domestic, to ascertain his name and place of habitation, she retired from the window, to her chamber, in evident perturbation of spirits. The servant punctually obeyed orders, and faithfully reported, that this flower of paradise, blossomed on the desert wild. Almira's natural hauteur, and acquired pride, were summoned, to expel this intruder on her prospects of high life. The attempt was fruitless. She had too long reposed on the downy couch of indolence, to enter on a conflict with the most potent passion of mortality.—The roses of health gradually faded from her cheek, the lustre of a piercing eye was obscured. Her frame imperceptibly verged towards decay. The advice of an eminent physician was requested. After listening to a recital of symptoms, which his penetration pronounced fallacious, he candidly declared Almira's real complaint, to be a concealed malady of the heart, which had long festered on the citadel of life, and must soon demolish the beautiful structure. Painful indisposition commonly triumphs over obstinate dissimulation. Advancing death levels his shafts at the crown of pride. Almira ingenuously confessed her ardent attachment to

Fidele; and added, that existence without him must forever be an insupportable burthen. Her parents' features brightened with a glow of hope at this pleasing discovery; and a horseman was immediately dispatched with the following letter.

Dear Sir,
If the happiness, if the life of parents, who feel with the most keen sensibility, for an only child, the darling hope of their aged days, can ought avail: If the health, the peace, of a once blooming, now languishing girl, whose bosom is the seat of spotless and for you, undivided affection, can possibly interest your heart: If the splendors of illimitable fortune, or prospects bright as the meridian sun can add a charm to life, let not this letter plead in vain. Almira has fixed her irreversible affections upon you; nothing can redeem her from the grave, but that indissoluble union, which may heaven sanction by a lengthened date of happy years. The chariot and four awaits your commands in the morning. The bearer has orders to deliver you bills to the amount of ten thousand pounds. We subscribe, in anticipation, your most tender parents,

J. B.
M. B.

The postilion rode express; his master told him that he was commissioned on life and death. He found Fidele at his little cottage; he was dressing himself to walk out with Zephyra. The day of their nuptials had been settled early that morning; it was to be on the morrow. The servant respectfully enquired his name and presented the letter, and bank notes. Fidele broke the seal, and perused the contents. A tear trickled down his cheek—a gentle sigh agitated his bosom. He was composed in a few minutes, and desiring the servant to be seated, returned for an answer.

Ever Honoured,
Respect, mingled with sincere affection, salutes the generous. The solemn sanction of my word is irrevocable. With the dawn of the morrow's sun I lead Zephyra, to the altar of my God. She's mine by love's eternal tie. The most fervent wishes of a heart, that bleeds for others woes, are tendered, to the fountains of benevolence, on your behalf. The notes are returned unopened. Acceptance, hesitation would be a crime. May the evening of your life be happy indeed. I have the honour to remain, your most affectionate friend,
Fidele.

The faithful shepherd, as he pressed the seal, stamped on the yielding way a falling tear. Angels themselves might wish to shed such tears. He wept not over gold. It was the dew of humanity, that distils the balm of compassion. For Fidele paused a moment, then reassumed the pen, and wrote the hapless maid.

My Amiable Friend,
A letter which I have this moment received from your worthy parents, has disclosed a painful and affecting secret; it is graven on my faithful bosom, and silent as the house of death, shall the sacred mansion remain. Unconscious to myself that the lovely, the now unhappy Almira, bloomed in the paradise of fortune, I pledged my heart to an object worthy of its purest regards; and previous to a knowledge of the tender sentiments that your bosom

fostered, my vows were registered in the archives of manly probity. I flatter myself that reason, and religion, will applaud my present determination. It is true, my amiable friend, that disappointed affection may speak another language: But Almira could have little hope of constancy, if Zephyra was sacrificed at the shrine of wealth. Philosophy administers poor opiates to the afflicted spirit. Human wisdom applies inefficacious remedies to the lacerated heart. There is a power that woundeth, it also healeth again. To that benignant comforter of sad distress I earnestly commend the sorrowing Almira; and may the genial influences of divine consolation, descend in softest showers of compassionate tenderness, and gently wear away the image of Fidele. A most delicate solicitude for thy returning health, thou lovely maid, will induce to frequent enquiries. The bloom of thy cheek, shall flourish on Zephyra's. The pale lily of death must wither the spring of joy, on the aspect of Fidele. Live, greatly, nobly live, for both.

Fidele

Almira, and her parents waited the servant's return with impatience. The reply affected them exceedingly. They mutually admired the greatness of his soul, whilst they lamented the settled refusal.

Fidele was united to Zephyra upon the morrow. His sensibility was too exquisite. The news of Almira's gradual decline, preyed hourly on a slender constitution. Zephyra caught the weakening contagion—and three celestial spirits sweetly languished into life together.

Oft shall the village maid with humble swain
   To Fidele's, faithful Fidele's grave repair

For truth and love, and honour's holy fane,
  And probity of soul—all center there.

Critical Commentary

"Fidele" belongs with other narratives published in *The Massachusetts Magazine*, as well as in other American magazines before 1800, to the tradition of sentimental Romanticism: The emphasis is on emotion and the manifestation of feelings. The sensitivity of the characters is strongly underscored: Flower images abound, and tears are shed at the appropriate moments. Herbert R. Brown argues that the sentimental tear invests a man with supernatural, celestial powers.[3] The figural constellation likewise mirrors the contemporary value system. Honest work and the satisfaction resulting from a simple rural life, as exemplified in the figure of the father, are propagated; city life, pride, and indulgence, as exemplified by Almira are depicted as fatal. "[R]ural virtue as opposed to urban vice" is a frequent theme of early magazine tales.[4] When they meet, two worlds collide, and their incompatibility can be read as precipitating the death of the three young protagonists.

The protagonists are not developed as literary characters. This is not necessary, since their generic names place them in a framework of referential familiarity with the sentimental: the Latin *fidelis*, meaning "faithful," even makes the title a pleonasm. The "Fidele" lines from Shakespeare's *Cymbeline*, plus "On Hearing a Lady Sing Fidele" by *Polydore*, provide an intertextual frame to the story (the texts are reprinted below). Aside from the similar-sounding "Fidelio" that is used as a *nom de plume* in the "Seat of the Muses" section of *The Massachusetts Magazine*, the intertextual quality of the name also tells the reader that at least the main character will not live to the end of the tale. Zephyra and Almira are not so deterministically loaded: a "Zaphira" appears as a princess in the anonymous "Concise History of the Algerines" in *The Massachusetts Magazine.* "Almira" appears to have been a favorite name for somewhat spoiled daughters.

In the story at hand, Fidele, Zephyra, and Almira form a classic love triangle which results in disaster. But there is more to the text. At the age of 19, the main character Fidele loses his father, an upright lawyer who always sought to contribute to the commonweal. Shortly after, Fidele falls in love with Zephyra, who is—in accordance with the last wish of his father—a "village maiden, rich in innocence alone." The antipode to this rural happiness is the figure of Almira, a daughter of a rich India merchant, who has irrevocably fallen for Fidele. But although Almira is about to die from a broken heart and Fidele is offered 10,000 pounds, he stays true to his word and marries Zephyra. The story ends with all three of them dead: Almira from unrequited love, and Fidele, invested with a very sensitive nature, from empathy, while Zephyra seems to die of natural causes, as far as tuberculosis can be called that.[5]

The apparent one-dimensionality of this sentimental *Liebestod* story, however, is subverted in the course of the events, mostly because the death of all three protagonists dissolves the fixity of the character constellation. Traditionally, the city girl not only falls prey to her vanity, but the principled American couple lives happily ever after.[6] In the modified context of "Fidele," textual elements like the monologue of the father, bordering on a sermon in its long-windedness, gains additional meaning. Also, the short insertion about "the deliverer of America" who holds a speech in "a neighbouring state" takes on added meaning as well.

The father seems at first sight not important for the development of the plot, but he is. For one, he is the figure who pleads with his son to marry a virtuous country girl. Usually in the sentimental story, the parents of the female protagonist arrange the marriage for their daughter. The reversal of the parents' role is one mark of an initial dissociation process from the British sentimental tradition. Furthermore, Fidele's parent is described as a father who hands down his republican principles to his son, in terms reminiscent of the prototypical American in the young republic. Not only is he said to renounce his earnings, as George Washington did (who was probably the best-known and most popular person in the United States at the time), he is also ascribed Republican virtues such as charity, justice, and self-denial. Americans who had gone to pre-war grammar school would have been familiar with the Roman classics, and the frequent printings of translations from Horace in *The Massachusetts Magazine* show that these texts formed part of the culture of the time.[7] By referring to him as "Horatio" then, he comes to emulate the antique model as a paragon of virtue for the young American republic.

The reference to George Washington is not as inconspicuous as it seems at first sight either. Washington was legend; he was ascribed all virtues commonly looked on as being absolutely necessary for maintaining a republic. The politician in the narrative is identified obliquely not by name but by a typical Washington epithet: "the deliverer of America."[8] Almost religious veneration of Washington was common in post-revolutionary America. His appearance in "Fidele" is of course constructed, but at the same time he is thus linked to the young man who goes to see and hear him speak. His appearance is in line with the stress on the virtues considered essential for American Republicanism in "Fidele," and it matches real political events: George Washington *did* visit most of the United States in the fall of 1789, which suggests that the story might be referring to a historical speech.[9]

The reference to Washington is not accidental, or merely decorative. There is, rather, a political level to "Fidele" which gains prominence as one considers the spirit of initiation and political change that swept through the newly founded United States during the late 1780s: Only two years before "Fidele" was published, the United States Constitution was introduced; the Bill of Rights, not yet signed by all states, but omnipresent in public discussion, accentuated the individuality, the liberty and the rights of every (white male) citizen.

With the historical background and the exemplary republican father in mind, a closer look at the character constellation uncovers the political allegory imposed upon the sentimental narrative: the young republic is portrayed as being exposed to the seductive impulses of a manipulative coloniser. If Fidele, his father, and Zephyra are the embodiment of the new Americans, then Almira and her family symbolically constitute the continuing threat to this new republicanism. The father, being an India merchant, is evocative of the British East India Company holding the trading monopoly with the colonies before the War of Independence. After all, *The Massachusetts Magazine* was published in Boston, whose harbour had been the setting of the Boston Tea Party in December 1773, in which American colonists took the tea that the British East India Company intended to import to America, and threw it overboard from the brig *Beaver*. The Tea Act, passed by British Parliament against American protest, allowed the East India Company to import tea from other colonies like China without paying taxes to Britain. This was perceived by the American colonists as yet another constriction of their rights and freedom.[10]

Almira herself is described in predominantly negative terms, redolent of the vices that were already recognized in ancient Rome as hazardous to the well-being of the republic: "hauteur," "pride" and "indolence" seal her fate; she is unable to detach herself from Fidele—just as Britain was unwilling to detach herself from the United States. This ultimately leads to her demise. The representative of America, however, who does not sell his principles, marries the rural American girl, for reasons of sentiment and fidelity. It is the continuing presence of the originally British attitudes, the luxury and the self-indulgence, that results in the destruction of all three. Thus, the seemingly tagged-on, romantic ending might have been intended as a political warning.

The death of all three figures could therefore be seen either as a concession to a strong tradition of sentimental tales at the time, or as a shift away from the moralising, instructive tales that still dominated the contemporary magazines. By integrating a political level of meaning into the text, "Fidele" moves toward the more complex and ambiguous literary format of the short story.

There are signs of a calculated brevity as well. The text remains short, although it covers a time span of at least several months and contains two focal themes: the life and death of Fidele's father, and the fatal love story of the three young people. Brevity is achieved through focus on dialogue and letters that communicate the hopes, feelings and reactions of the protagonists rather than on the events themselves.

With the subtitle pronouncing the story "An American Tale," Caloc falls in with contemporary attempts at demarcating the beginning of a literary emancipation from Britain. However, one cannot help observing that the clumsy introduction of specifically American elements to "Fidele" does not keep step with the tone and the sentimental conventions that still adhere to European models. However, the function of American literary texts of the period was at least in part the creation of an autochthonous cultural voice that attempted to aid the consolidation of the young republic.

Nadine Kraus, Patricia Landvogt

APPENDICES

Fidele: A Favourite Song

The text was printed in the "Seat of the Muses" section of the *Massachusetts Magazine,* November 1790. The lyrics are taken from *Cymbeline,* though the play is not identified as the source in the text.

I.
To fair Fidele's grassy tomb,
Soft maids and village hinds shall bring,
Each op'ning sweet of earliest bloom,
And rifle all the breathing spring.
Each op'ning sweet of earliest bloom,
And rifle all the breathing spring.

II.
No wailing ghost shall dare appear
To vex with shrieks this quiet grove,
But shepherd lads assemble here
And melting virgins own their love.

III.
No wither'd witch shall here be seen,
No goblins lead their nightly crew,
The female fays shall haunt the green
And dress thy grave with pearly dew.

IV.
The red breast oft at evening hours
Shall kindly lend his little aid,
With hoary moss and gather'd flow'rs
To deck the ground where thou art laid.

V.
When howling winds and beating rain
In tempest shake the sylvan cell,
Amidst the chase on ev'ry plain,
The tender thought on thee shall dwell.

VI.
Each lonely scene shall thee restore
For thee the tear be duly shed,
Belov'd till life can charm no more
And mourn'd 'till pity's self be dead.

On Hearing a Lady Sing Fidele

The text was printed in the "Seat of the Muses" section of the *Massachusetts Magazine,* November 1791.

Fair Delia sings Fidele's death,
The sound bespeaks despair;
She fills with pain, by her soft breath,
The sympathetick air.

She sings; and while her plaintive strain
Lights gently on the ear;
The feeling eye can ne'er restrain
A tributary tear.

> From her kind lips, Fidele's charms
> A heighten'd worth derive;
> The song, with love each heart alarms,
> Yet keeps distress alive.
>
> In deserts safe might Delia rest,
> Nor fear the uncultur'd crew;
> Her voice would soothe the savage breast,
> And all its rage subdue.
>
> Polydore

Notes

[1] Philenia, a name that seems to stand in the tradition of Greek and Latinate pseudonyms yet without a linguistic basis in either language, was a *nom de plume* of Sarah Wentworth Morton. Its appearance in the story suggests at least a literary friendship between Caloc and Morton.

[2] This "almost religious veneration" identifies the visitor as George Washington. Two months earlier, in March 1791, *The Massachusetts Magazine* published "Sketches of the President of the United States" with a typical description of Washington: "Most nations have been favoured with some patriotic deliverer ... but these illustrious heroes, though successful in preserving and defending, did not like Washington, form or establish empires, which will, in all probability, be the refuge or asylum of liberty, banished from Europe by luxury and corruption."

[3] Herbert R. Brown, "Elements of Sensibility in the Massachusetts Magazine," *American Literature* 1.3 (1929): 291.

[4] Eugene Current-Garcia, *The American Short Story before 1850: A Critical History* (Boston: Twayne, 1985): 5.

[5] Characters in other stories published in the textual environment of "Fidele" are also consumed by their sensibility; in fact, Herbert Brown has drawn up an extensive sensibility death-toll in his "Elements of Sensibility," 293–94.

[6] Leslie A. Fiedler, *Love and Death in the American Novel* (London: Jonathan Cape, 1967): 62.

[7] Numerous translations of Horace's works appeared in *The Massachusetts Magazine* before, with, and after "Fidele."

[8] That this was a standard procedure of the time is attested to by William A. Bryan in his preface to *George Washington in American Literature* (New York: Columbia UP, 1952): vii–viii.

[9] Washington toured through all states except Vermont and Rhode Island, which at that time were not yet members of the union.

[10] Donald Ross, *American History & Culture* (New York: Peter Lang, 2000): 60.

The Story of the Captain's Wife
and an Aged Woman
Ruri Colla

"The Story of the Captain's Wife and an Aged Woman" appeared in the October and November 1789 issues of the second series of the Gentlemen and Ladies Town and Country Magazine, *published in Boston by Nathaniel Coverly.*[1] *The author of the story signed his or her name as "Ruri Colla" which can be translated from Latin as "tiller of the soil." However, the name of the author has so far not been discovered.*

With its mixture of seemingly supernatural elements, sexual innuendo, and the happy ending reconciling the Captain and his wife, this story has attracted the attention of more contemporary scholars and anthologists of short stories than any other story in this collection, with the exception of Irving's "Adventure of the German Student." It has also received praise for making use of "a great deal of fictional skill, a craftsmanship quite beyond the norm for the age."[2] *While the editors also include the text in this collection of early short stories, closer analysis reveals that the "craftsmanship" is the result of a blend of different short prose types that were common at the end of the 18th century, particularly the tale, the essay, and the sermon.*

The Story of the Captain's Wife and an Aged Woman

For the Gentlemen and Ladies Magazine.

Mr Coverly,

There is not perhaps in the whole system of vices any one to which human nature is more prone than this, viz. the censuring and condemning others for those very things which we practise ourselves; and 'tis no very uncommon thing, to see a person suffer his resentment to rise to an exceeding high pitch against his neighbour for treating him, or only a suspicion that he has treated him, in the same way that he himself has before treated that very same person and for which he has never felt himself disposed to make any kind of satisfaction: but this must be as wrong as it is common; for not withstanding it is wrong in A to injure B, after that B has injured A, yet B has no right to entertain any resentment against A, when he has conducted in the same manner towards him, and has made him no kind of satisfaction therefore; or at least such a resentment must fit with an exceeding ill grace on B, and prove the exceeding criminality of his conduct, it being what he most pointedly condemns himself. People would do well to consider before they are so lavish with their censures of others, to pause a moment, and ask themselves this serious question, "do not I practise the same things myself, for which I am just going to load my neighbour with the reproaches? If this idea could be reduced to practise it would have two very good effects;

one is, scandal would in a measure, cease to be the topics of conversation; the other is, many people would leave off the practise of certain vices, that they might have the opportunity of exposing the follies of others.

I have no where met with a more striking instance of the above-mentioned vice than in the following narration, which I some years ago had from a then aged clergyman of this Commonwealth, and which, though some parts of it appear of the incredible kind, yet he affirmed it to have been fact, and that it took place while he was at his studies, before he entered on the work of the ministry, in one of the capital towns on the American Continent, where he had his place of abode; the story I believe was never before committed to print, which consideration has induced me to insert it here. [3]

A woman of the age of about twenty-one years, the wife of a sea-captain (whose husband had been absent on a voyage, a very considerable time longer than he was expected he would have been gone when he left his home) began to be exceedingly anxious for his safety, and as a succession of days and weeks brought her no intelligence of him, she grew quite inconsolable. Day after day, she spent her time walking down on the different wharves, inquiring of all who had lately arrived, if they had any tidings from her husband, fruitless were all her enquiries, which fixed a solemn gloom on her countenance.

One day as she was returning from her unavailing enquiries, she met an aged woman, who looking steadfastly in her face, said, "Child what makes you appear so melancholy?" The afflicted woman told her it was the absence of her husband, whom she never expected to see more. The old woman perceiving the depth of her distress spoke smilingly to her saying, "Child be not so troubled; your husband is alive, he is well; in time he will return in safety; follow my advice; say nothing; you meet me on THAT wharf this evening a little before the close of the day light, and you shall see your husband, and be returned to this place before morning."

The woman was struck with amazement at this proposal: and though she gave but a small degree of credence to the assertion, yet her desire was so great to see him, that her wishes got the better of her belief, and she promised to meet the old woman accordingly; on which they parted; and the wife retired to her home.

After returning home she began to ruminate on what was past, and the whole appeared to her so strange, that she concluded to pay no regard to the appointment; yet when the time appointed came, her desires prevailed upon her to repair to the place appointed, where she no sooner arrived than she met the old woman with a half-bushel measure under her arm. "Follow me," said she, and stepping through between two stores to the backside of the wharf, she put the half-bushel into the water, which was immediately transformed to a sail boat, with the sails all standing; the old woman taking her by the hand led her into the boat, they shoved off from the wharf, a smart breeze springing up, they soon lost sight of the town, the harbour and the land. The consternation of the lady was such at this adventure, that she was nearly in a suspension of ideas, but according to her best judgement in about two hour's time they made an harbour, on which a fine town was situated, they landed at a wharf, and walked up a street about ten rods, when the old woman turning up to a door, said to the lady in a low voice, "here child is your husband, in this house, go in, you will find him—meet me two hours before day, at the boat.

Story of the Captain's Wife

The lady, full of astonishment entered the house, where, to her increased surprise, she beheld her husband, sitting at the table at supper. He cast his eyes upon her, and viewed her with the greatest degree of attention, while eating his supper, during which, his wife observed in his hand a knife and a fork, of a very curious and singular form.

Supper being finished, he arose from the table and took a seat by her, saying woman; perhaps my conduct may appear odd, and perhaps offensive to you—but I trace in your countenance every feature of my wife; I therefore propose spending the night with you, if it is in my power to purchase the favour, I wish therefore you would inform me of your terms. The lady blushing replied, this is a negotiation which I am totally unacquainted with, yet Sir, if you will deliver me the curious knife and fork, with which you eat your supper, I will grant you, your request. He told her the knife and fork were of insignificant value indeed—he could not hesitate of giving her one hundred times the value of them. But the knife and fork he wished to keep, on account of an intimate friend, who had made a present of them. But the woman insisted they were her only terms, which if he did not mean to comply with, she hoped he would give her no more trouble on the occasion. He feeling she was determined, gave her the knife and fork, on which they retired.

At two or three hours before day, the husband falling asleep, she arose softly, left the house, and repaired to the boat, where she met the old woman, they entered on board, and in about two or three hours time were at the wharf, from whence they first sailed, being then between half break of day, and the rising of the sun, from whence they returned to her own house.

About seven months from this her husband returned into port and before he reached his house some officious friend informed him of the pregnancy of his wife.

Words are scarcely capable of conveying an idea of the rage into which he flew in this occasion, he stamped and stormed like a mad-man, swearing by all that was great or good, that he would never let his eyes on her again—that a breach of the marriage covenant—that incontinency was a crime in its nature unpardonable, and which never could be forgiven.

Second Part

That he would as fast as possible make sale of his estate—leave his native country, and return no more—That he would leave the unfaithful partner of his bed, to the free and full possession of her favourite, or else satisfy with the heart's blood of them both.

However, he took lodgings at a friend's house, and so vigilant was he, that his wife's inconsistent attempts to fall in his company, all proved fruitless. Day after day did she rack her inventions in fabricating schemes to bring herself into his company, but all to no kind of effect.

More than a week had transpired when she went to an uncle of his, and agreed with him to make an entertainment, and that her husband should be one of his guests, and she was to be there incog. until the guests had sat down at table. The guests were invited and accepted—the day arrived—the guests made their appearance, dinner was brought upon the table; those who were bidden sat down.—It so happened that our sea-Captain had a plate sat before him which was unaccompanied with a knife and fork. Notice was taken of it by the master of the feast, who called on a waiter to supply the Captain, when on a sudden from a door right behind him, issued his wife, and laid in his plate the remarkable knife and fork which she received of him in the foreign port.

The Captain seeing the knife and fork, recognized them in a moment, which summoned up nearly the whole mass of his blood into his face, and by his looks there was the utmost danger of its bursting through the skin—from the vivid colour of the rose, his face assumed the lifeless colour of the lily, which again was charged to the blooming red, and thus alternately did his countenance assume different aspects.

It was some time before his confusion would admit of his speaking, at length he arose from the table (while the company neglected the plentiful provision which was made for them, to gaze upon the Captain, and turning round to his wife, he thus addressed her: "Pray, in the name of goodness, inform me where you procured this remarkable knife and fork?" Do you wish (reply'd his wife) I should satisfy your curiosity at this time? "Yes, by all means," (reply'd he) Well, then, said the wife, do you not remember that between seven and eight months ago, you in a foreign port, parted with such a knife and fork to a woman, for the sake of her company a night? The Captain in confusion, after some hesitation, answered in affirmative. Well, said the wife, "that woman was no other than she who addresses you," with that she gave them a relation of the whole adventure. The Captain, (whose confusion rather increased) stood motionless for a few moments, while the company was all attention—at length he broke silence and thus addressed her: "Dear, loving and much injured wife, with the deepest contrition I now make you my double acknowledgements, first, for the incontinence which I in my heart was actually guilty of towards you; and secondly, for my ill-usage of you for the false suspicion of a crime which I myself was in fact guilty of—I hope you will treat me in a different way from that in which I have conducted towards you, and overlook that real guilt which I had proposed never to have acquitted you of. I am myself a guilty culprit, convicted by your own confession.—I lye wholly at your mercy, and I hope you will extend that clemency towards me which I deny'd to you.—The wife with a softness peculiar to herself, answered him, Tho' your conduct to me (all things considered) has been rather hard-hearted, yet I have no disposition to act the same or unfeeling part towards you—you have my hearty forgiveness, since matters are as they are; and I hope from this you will not again take it upon yourself to divorce yourself from your wife without first examining whether she is guilty or not, and never hereafter to condemn another for these practices which you follow yourself.

The company was exceedingly pleased with her answer—another seat and plate was provided—they all sat down and made a very merry, as well as a very good dinner; after which they arose in good humour, each one repairing to his respective home—the Captain and his wife to theirs, and nothing more was said by either of them with regard to the unaccountable adventure of theirs.

Whether the foregoing relation was true in fact, or not, I pretend not to say, (tho' the character of the relater was well established in the moral world) yet it strongly enforces the observations made in the foregoing part of this paper, and every one would do well to consider, that while he condemns others for those things which he practices himself, he cuts the same ridiculous and despicable figure with the Captain, in the foregoing narrative; and that when at any time he has been exposing the vices of his neighbours, he should conclude with this observation, I am the man; and he may rest assured, that if he does not make the observation himself, those in the company will not fail to do it, if they are acquainted with him.

Critical Commentary

Jack B. Moore called the "Story of the Captain's Wife and an Aged Woman" one of the rare "non-comic native fictions" that appeared in an American magazine in the 18th century.[4] Eugene Current-Garcia and Bert Hitchcock applaud the author for the "use of irony, novel detail, both realistic and fantastic, a matter-of-fact tone, and a touch of macabre—all of which lead to remarkably contrasting conclusions."[5] However, neither Moore nor Current-Garcia and Hitchcock have made any specific comments on the genre issue as far as this story is concerned. A more careful analysis of the text reveals that the story is an amalgam of various short prose types: tale, essay, and sermon.

There is a clear division into an outer frame and an interior narrative. The narrative shows characteristics of the tale: an episodic structure following a simple plot, involving rather generic figures and including several folk motifs. The frame shows signs of the argumentative essay, a format found in British sources as early as the 16th century and familiar to readers of magazines at least since the 1740s.[6] Within this format, the text also shows similarities to the sermon, with a theoretical frame based on a biblical question and an interior tale exemplifying the moral and religious problem, plus a conclusion that integrates them. To a certain extent, the interior tale follows the format of the typical exemplum from the sermonic tradition.

One of the characterizing features of the sermon exemplum is that it "has a lack of interest in character."[7] Accordingly, the three main characters indicated in the title are not individualized by name but characterized by social position, personality, gender, and conduct. The same lack of individuation, however, is typical of the folktale, and the characters' actions as well as their behavior identify them as types rather than as individualized figures.

The sea captain is the typical absent husband of the folktale tradition. As usual for men at the time, he is the one earning the money, and he supposes himself superior to women in all situations of life. So after committing adultery in at least one foreign port, he is still confident of his irreproachable conduct upon returning home, and only confesses his fault after being confronted with physical evidence. Also, the motif of the husband making love to his wife without knowing that it is her is a stock motif in both folktales and in literary texts.[8]

His young wife is depicted as the loving, caring, and obedient woman. And she is justly rewarded for her faithfulness in spite of the long absence of her husband and her longing for him. Her superior cleverness is made obvious through her insistence on being given the knife and fork her husband is using in eating supper before she spends the night with him.

The figure of the aged woman introduces a supernatural element. She is the kind helper of the young woman because she makes it possible for her to see her husband for one night, without asking anything in return. Her magic not only transforms the half-bushel measure into a boat, it also collapses space, if not time—the captain's wife has to be back at the wharf at the appointed hour. She returns punctually with the knife and fork which turn into requisites for the unfaithful husband's undoing.

Even though there are several folktale motifs distributed throughout the text, and even though folktales combine entertaining and educational purposes, the "Story of the Captain's Wife and an Aged Woman" is not exactly a folktale—or rather, it does not appear in a typical format. The textual environment of the preceding and following frame narrative makes an identification as a folktale difficult.

The frame narrative in turn does not appear in the standard format of a sermon. The frame text contains a moral discussion of a problem that can be identified as simultaneously philosophical, legal, and religious: "the censuring and condemning of others for those very things which we practise ourselves." In the Bible, this motif is exemplified on several occasions, most prominently in the first chapter of the Gospel according to St. Matthew: "Judge not, that ye not be judged. Forwith what judgement ye judge, ye will be judged: and with what measure ye mete, it shall be measured to you again. And why beholdest thou the mote that is in thy brother's eye, but considerest not the beam that is in thine own eye?"[9] To use variables like A and B is of course not an exceedingly clever literary device. They create a curious construction: writing a moral tale rather than a sermon—where it would have been appropriate—Ruri Colla apparently did not want to make the reference to the biblical motif too obvious. At the same time, there is no legal title or issue that would cover the same ground, so the problem appears in a transformed format, not quite a legal question but not quite a philosophical issue either. Finally, the sermonic background is clearly visible in the presence of the old clergyman as the source of the story.

The same clergyman serves another purpose: Were it not for him, the story could be read as a fairy tale, or worse, as a tale of witchcraft. And while it is important to note that literature of the late 18th century did not necessarily equate witchcraft with evil, the figure of the old woman would at least have appeared ambiguous.[10] Of course there is no other way that the captain's wife could have become pregnant from her husband by natural means; only the appearance of the old woman, not motivated otherwise, makes it possible for the young lady to travel a distance across the sea in one night that later takes her husband seven months to cover.

The supernatural powers that the old woman brings into the text are used in accordance with Robert Doran's description of the functionality of the fantastic or supernatural in the short story "to produce a specific but well defined effect, or to enable the author to achieve goals which would have otherwise been difficult or impossible."[11] In this context, it is important to see that the young woman's legally and morally sound pregnancy is of course absolutely necessary for the moral intent of the story: The story must prevent a misidentification of the wife as an adulteress; this, however, can only be achieved through means that even the late 18th century reader would probably have read as non-realistic. Eugene Current-Garcia has offered a somewhat sarcastic analysis of a type of early magazine story that clearly includes "The Story of the Captain's Wife and an Aged Woman":

> Early tale writers often became pseudomoralists themselves. To justify their role as storytellers, they wrote fiction that resembled the Biblical parables evoked by the clergy, combining under the cloak of sermonic truth-telling many scandalous episodes or sequences of events that could be luridly embroidered.[12]

Current-Garcia's sarcasm seems justified in view of the fact that even with the backing by the clergyman, and in view of its obviously moral intent, the story remains lurid, and loaded with sexual innuendo: The young woman is not content with learning that he husband is alive, but her urge to see him is also caused by sexual desire. The husband does not legally commit adultery, since he sleeps, after all, with his own wife, though morally he does, since to him the woman only resembles his wife. The wife's role is not as innocent as it may appear: She sleeps with her husband even though he is clearly unaware of her identity. The old woman, lastly, serves as a somewhat dubious matchmaker, dropping off the captain's wife in the seedy part of a foreign seaport where, unaccompanied by a male or female chaperone, she must of course be misidentified as a streetwalker.

This does not mean that on the level of the home town (most likely Boston) the Captain's wife is not the typical picture of the virtuous female. But she is not only a loving faithful wife, she is also clever enough not to forget to ensure that she can prove her innocence and chastity. The story does not go so far as to challenge the distribution of gender roles, for the typical woman had to be pious, considerate, religious, compassionate, and representitive of virtue at home. Moreover, being a mother was the highest fulfillment for a woman. These virtues, and the desire for motherhood, are all found in the young wife.

The constructed situation of the pregnant wife of an absentee husband mirrored an area of societal experience, and expectations, that usually led to the ostracizing of the "guilty" woman while men were tacitly granted the leeway of a double standard, creating separate cultural areas for men that enabled them to have extramarital sex. The story presented here thus criticizes not only the husband's self-righteousness as addressed in the frame narrative, but the very double standard. When the wife forgives her husband, she not only temporarily assumes a position of power which she is shown to use with grace and deliberation, her very situation as a typical figure rather than as an individual can be read as a challenge to the distribution of power in the marital situation.

In this light, the use of the clearly supernatural aged woman takes on an additional level of potential meaning: Witch or para-angelic helper in the folktale and exemplum traditions, she does not have a parallel in the sentimental fiction of the period that usually told the stories of fallen women and errant wives. Thus there is of course the possibility for readers—male readers, assumedly—to reject the story out of hand as purely fictional and even fantastic.

The narrative perspective is of additional importance in this context. The first person narrator of this story does not claim veracity for the story. In fact, the formulation whether the "foregoing relation was true in fact, or not, I pretend not to say, (tho' the character of the relater was well established in the moral world)" is highly ironic, since the Captain's moral character was just as well established, until his wife produced the knife and fork. The narrative reduction of the distance between narrator and reader is also a cleverly designed disclaimer concerning the truth-value of the story, turning the attention at the end of the text appropriately enough to the religious question again, which forms the story's frame at the beginning. In the light of this question, however, it does not really matter whether the story of the Captain's wife can make any claims to truth or not, the point being that nobody should pass judgment if he or she is guilty of the same sin, or crime—a conclusion that casts a somewhat slanting shadow on the status of marital fidelity in the late 18th century United States.

The question whether or not "The Story of the Captain's Wife and an Aged Woman" should be included among the short stories is not as easily answered as Moore, Current-Garcia and Hitchcock, and even Nagel claim. But it is included here because of the combinatory effect that arises from the mixture of folktale elements, a sermon, with an essay frame, allusions to the exemplum format, and aspects of sentimental fiction. In their combination, the parts are irreducible to just one format, but as a combination, and given the ability of the novel as well as of its younger sibling the short story to adapt and assimilate all other forms of narrative prose, the description as an early short story seems justified.

Its *American* character can also be established. The American setting in a "capital town on the American continent" is at least potentially identifiable as Boston by its seaport and by the place of publication of the magazine. The plot is not necessarily American, and unlike in the "Story of Julia," the characters are not noticeably Americanized. However, the narrator's insistence on the originality of the story when he writes that "the story I believe was never before committed to print" is reinforced by the direct address to the magazine "For the Gentlemen and Ladies Magazine" and its publisher "Mr. Coverly." This format is possibly used in analogy to the practice of *The Massachusetts Magazine,* which distinguished original contributions by the notice "For The Massachusetts Magazine" or "To the editor" from pirated stories. Also, even though "Ruri Colla" has so far not been identified, the rural pose expressed in the *nom de plume* makes this story even more likely an original piece of native American fiction.

Ines Dreßler, Susanne Heiden, Alexandra Rägle

Notes

[1] Both series of the magazine were short-lived even by standards of the time.
[2] James Nagel, *Anthology of the American Short Story* (Boston: Houghton Mifflin, 2007): 48.
[3] The Commonwealth referred to is likely Massachusetts. Depending on how "capital" is interpreted, this could refer to a variety of seaports, including Boston.
[4] Jack B. Moore, "Native Elements in American Magazine Short Fiction, *1741–1800*." Diss. Univ. of North Carolina, 1963: 246.
[5] Eugene Current-Garcia and Bert Hitchcock, eds., *American Short Stories* (New York: Longman, 1996): 5.
[6] Barbara Korte, *The Short Story in Britain* (Tübingen: UTB Francke, 2003): 24–25.
[7] Larry Scanlon, *Narrative, Authority, and Power: The Medieval Exemplum and the Chaucerian Tradition* (Cambridge, MA: Cambridge UP, 1994): 60.
[8] Cf. Antti Aarne and Stith Thompson, *The Types of the Folk Tales* (Helsinki: FF Communications, 1961): 305.
[9] Matthew 7:1–3.
[10] Roy Porter, "Witchcraft and Magic in Enlightenment, Romantic and Liberal Thought," *Witchcraft and Magic in Europe: The Eighteenth and Nineteenth Centuries*, eds. Bengt Ankarloo and Stuart Clark (Philadelphia: U of Pennsylvania P, 1999): 209–10.
[11] Robert Doran, "The Fantastic Tale: Poe and Scott," *Tale, Novella, Short Story: Currents in Short Fiction,* eds. Wolfgang

Görtschacher and Holger Klein (Tübingen: Stauffenburg Verlag, 204): 51.

[12] Current-García, Hitchcock, *American Short Stories*: 4.

Something Unaccountable
Z. P.

Jack B. Moore considered "Something Unaccountable" one of the best early American short stories not only because of its distinctly American setting, but also because he felt that its ingenious structure made it "aesthetically satisfying."[1] It was first printed in September 1789 in The Massachusetts Magazine. *Unfortunately, the identity of the author has not been discovered so far. Edward Pitcher anthologized "Something Unaccountable" in the American Gothic and Horrific Tales section of his collection.[2] He also lists one reprint of the text in the* New Hampshire and Vermont Magazine and General Repository, *with two minor alterations: the protagonist Mr. B. is replaced by a Mr. R., possibly only because of the illegibility of the letter B. in the issue of* The Massachusetts Magazine, *and the author's initials are changed to "O. M."—but again, there is as yet no identification for whom this might have been. Still, because of its refusal to explain, or to moralize, "Something Unaccountable" is one of the most fascinating early short stories, and a link to the established format of the later 19th century.*

Something Unaccountable

To the editors of The Massachusetts Magazine

Gentlemen,
The following Account, however incredible, is matter of serious fact, and never appeared in print. I flatter myself it will be entertaining.

Z. P.

Mr. B. had received a learned education at one of the first seminaries in America. The dawn of childhood displayed uncommon traits of genius; and the morn of manhood returned him to his respectable friends, all that the fondest affection could wish. Early designed for the law, he soon became distinguished at the bar, and blest with a handsome fortune, exerted all his abilities in defending the widow, and protecting the fatherless. Villany shrunk abashed from his penetrating eye; and the lawless oppressor trembled as he spoke. His manners were engaging to the highest degree. His morals irreproachable in the commerce with both sexes; his piety resulted from gratitude and love. The conscience void of offence, seldom feels the gloom of superstition; perhaps no man was freer from the least tincture of it, than this worthy character, and although a warm advocate for the agency of Providence, he frequently smiled at the vulgar notions of those extraordinary appearances which are deemed supernatural. A few years had rolled imperceptibly away, in performing continual acts of benevolence, and doing illimited good to such as had none to help, when some special pleadings in a momentous cause obliged him to undertake a journey of eighty miles. Business of various kinds delayed his setting out till the last day of term approached; he mounted his horse before sunrise, travelled with expedition, and at eight in the evening reached within ten miles of his intended tour. Excessively fatigued by the heat of a violent August sun, he seriously wished for repose, and called at a minister's house to whom he had letters, and who rather kept genteel lodgings for men of science, than a caravansary for general refreshment.[3] The stranger was received with uncommon attentions, past a few moments in agreeable conversation—partook of a light supper—and retired to an elegant chamber. All nature was hush as the temple of death; not a voice to interrupt the calmness of repose; not a breath from the trees to disturb sleep; the family and servants were sunk in the arms of slumber; a universal solemn stillness pervaded the town; but neither wearisome lassitude, nor a predisposition for rest, were of any avail— Mr. B. turned from side to side, and as the hours past off grew more wakeful. A neighbouring church clock had struck twelve—the moon rose, and shed her fair influence around. He looked towards the door, and saw approaching his bed, a most beautiful girl about ten or fifteen. The elegance of her countenance, symmetry of limbs, and delicacy of shape, bespoke something more than human. It was a face he never had seen—the serenity of hope, the glow of faith, the rapture of joy, played upon features divinely expressive; yet her attitude was such, as displayed peculiar affection for him, and deeply interested the tenderest feelings. Her head gently inclined, her arms stretched out as to clasp a beloved object, awakened every emotion of compassion; and a visible languor that succeeded a healthy look—a deadly pallidness, that obliterated the fading rose, rendered this unexpected interview exquisitely affecting. He viewed her for some time with fixed attention, blended with the diffidence of beholding an angel in distress; drew the curtain on that side, and turned silently away. Again the appearance met his wondering sight, if possible, ten times more engaging than before. He had leisure to contemplate her dress, the animation that beamed from her eyes—the lovely ringlet of auburn tresses that flowed on her bosom. The *toute ensemble* surpassed description. Convinced that his door was carefully locked, and no other aperture leading to the chamber, he put on his clothes, and determined to traverse the town till morn. The unknown fair, attended to the stair case—and instantly vanished; with a look that expressed filial affection, and asked parental pity.

Various attempts to solve the inexplicable enigma busied his thoughts; he was assured it must be supernatural; the why and wherefore he could not fathom. Unwilling to hurt the feelings of the good old couple, he returned before they were up, called for his horse, settled the bill, took not the least notice of any thing extraordinary to the servant, and proceeded on his journey. A few days terminated the business in which he was engaged; a few more he resolved to dedicate to those friends who had honoured him with pleasurable invitations. The accomplishments of this excellent young man were a passport to the politest circles; among others, his Excellency the Governor who resided in the capital where he then was requested his company at dinner. Miss Amelia, his youngest daughter, bore a striking resemblance to the lovely form he had so lately seen; ten thousand confused ideas rushed upon his soul—he fell violently in love with this amiable lady, and previously to leaving the metropolis, made those honourable proposals which end in matrimony. Some intervening circumstances debarred him for two or three years the pleasure he sought for in a partner. At length the nuptials were consummated, and Madam B. retired with her husband, to the place of his abode. The returning twelvemonth crowned the wishes of the new married couple with an infant daughter, the peculiar favourite of a fond father; the darling of an affectionate mother. Four or five annual revolutions lead us to forget many things that once affected with a peculiar pathos. This was the case with Mr. B. From a practising attorney, he had passed to the grade of a barrister; from the bar, he had been summoned to the bench; and scarcely a trait of the fair one, whom he had once thought of with such various emotions, ever entered his mind. The little Amelia had nearly completed her ninth year; pronounced the paragon of beauty, and phoenix of accomplishments. Her grandfather (who still retained his post in government) wished to see her, and strongly advised her passing a few months with Madam—, the hostess of the house where Mr. B. formerly put up, who since that period had founded an Academy for young ladies, and was justly celebrated as the first preceptress in that state.[4] Every trace of a transaction which took place thirteen years before, had past off as the remembrance of a dream. The parents gave their consent, and Miss Amelia was put under the tuition of this incomparable governess. The writer of the present anecdote had the pleasure to be introduced to her at his Excellency's, and must in justice observe, that when imagination has taken the boldest flight—fancy collected every idea of perfection—judgement refined the whole—and genius drawn the most finished picture, it will fall infinitely short of her real portrait. Her external, from head to foot, was precisely the same, that I conceive Eve's to have been previous to the fall—her mind a degree above it, it was angelic, etherial, not a particle of earth belonged to the celestial inhabitant.

But a few weeks elapsed, and Amelia was seized with the alarming symptoms of a putrid fever.[5] All the physicians of eminence were instantly summoned; they candidly pronounced her case beyond the reach of art. An express was dispatched for Mrs. and Mr. B. They posted as on the wings of the wind. At the moment he entered the chamber, (that very one where so long before he had seen the appearance already mentioned) Miss Amelia was standing nearly in the attitude above described, supported by two attendants, whilst others were changing the bed. Her father looked—the whole transaction rushed upon his mind; he burst into agonizing tears; and fervently exclaimed, "Thy will be done, oh my God![6] and the God of my fathers! It was she whom I saw; help is in vain; I resign thee, sweet inhabitress of etherial realms! Thou wast lent for a moment, that hour is eternally past!" The third day from his arrival, she was no more. And I have frequently heard him say, that he recognized perfectly in his beloved daughter, the features and dress of the vision that appeared, whilst as yet he had no idea of marriage. And by comparing the minutes of the time when he undertook the journey heretofore spoken of, ascertained to a certainty, that the night of Miss Amelia's death completed fourteen years to an hour, from the moment of her first appearance to him, which was nearly five anniversaries previous to her having had existence.

Critical Commentary

There are a number of textual elements that identify "Something Unaccountable" as at least potentially American. Authorship, though not identifiable beyond the claim that "Something Unaccountable" had been "sent by Z. P.," or by "O. M.," is more likely to have been American than British, because texts pilfered from British sources usually went without any indication of authorship in the years following the War of Independence, while short prose of American origin often came with a *nom de plume* or at least, as in this case, initials.

Locality, though likewise not conclusively establishing American authorship, is another important feature. Mr. B is said to have been educated at "one of the first seminaries in America," and to have returned to his friends later, so readers would naturally resume that the rest of the story also takes place in America. Also, later Mr. B is invited to dine with "his Excellency the Governor who resided in the capital where he then was." There is no way telling *which* capital, but readers of *The Massachusetts Magazine* would have assumed that this naturally referred to Boston, while readers in other states could have felt equally entitled to relocate the story in their respective states.

As the opening paragraph reveals, the protagonist is a well-educated and intelligent lawyer who uses his legal skills mainly for the defense of widows and orphans. Even more so, he is a man of highest morals, completely untainted by common corruptions of the human mind. In other words, he is an American republican—not necessarily a typical Calvinist in that the element of economic success is conspicuously absent, but nonetheless a righteous and hard-working man who, like the father of "Fidele" (see above), uses his gifts for the good of those who need his support most.[7] Given that two main characteristics of Calvinism are the ideas of God being all-governing, and man being free at the same time, the story can be interpreted as being about an individual who has to cope with God's judgment even though it may appear incomprehensible. The incomprehensibility of the story, the lack of a visible cause and effect relation, and the unavoidability and resignation that come with the death of the perfect girl are a sort of "unity of effect" achieved by means of various interlocking motifs. Based on these motifs, contradictory and even mutually exclusive interpretations become possible.

"Something Unaccountable" makes use of a remarkable number of gothic elements, despite its publication in 1789, when what would later be called "American Gothic" was yet in the process of finding a form. Nonetheless, this story has a very gothic atmosphere and feeling, even though it omits several motifs nowadays considered central to gothic story telling.

The typically gothic sense of foreshadowing and anticipation first becomes apparent in the following lines:

> although a warm advocate for the agency of Providence, he frequently smiled at the vulgar notions of those extraordinary appearances which are deemed supernatural.

Any reader familiar with horror tales will immediately recognize the unavoidability of some supernatural phenomenon, or apparition, following this statement. Throughout the rest of the text, there are multiple repetitions of the word "supernatural." The most unusual element in the story, by contemporary as well as by today's standards, is the apparition of the ghost of the young girl. Usually ghosts appear, influence, and torment other figures in the stories they inhabit after the living characters they resemble have died. However, in this remarkable case the ghost actually appears *before* its earthly body comes into existence. Furthermore, the apparition does not trouble or scare Mr. B., which is rather uncommon. In fact, the apparition of the ghost does not create the daunting and uncanny atmosphere pervading the story; it is the lack of explanation for the phenomenon that does.

Other motifs of the gothic are more in line with the conventional format: "Something Unaccountable" for the most part takes place in a "minister's house" with a nearby church. Adding to the gothic experience, the church's bells strike twelve o'clock, creating the perfect atmosphere for a supernatural apparition. However, the house does not seem to be haunted on a more regular basis; that is, the apparition is not a resident ghost, but seems to have to do with Mr. B., whereas later American Gothic usually draws on architecture, especially churches and English-style country houses.

Some of the gothic elements can be used to make a case for the assumed Americanness of the story: "All nature was hush as the temple of death, . . . not a breath from the trees to disturb sleep." The passage can be read as an example of early Frontier Gothic: Nature becomes something disturbing and dangerous, a motif frequently used in American literature up to this day.[8] However, the metaphor "temple of death" sticks out as it seems out of place; it is possible that the origin of this idea can be traced to Central American architecture such as the temple-pyramids and cenotes of Chichén Itzá which were actually used for human sacrifices.

Depending on the interpretation of the apparition itself, another gothic motif can be identified. There seems to be an initial sexual attraction between grown man and childlike apparition, and thus an indication of a gothic motif of an incestuous relationship and even of paedophilia, the "most beautiful girl" looking as if she was "about ten or fifteen"—a remarkably inaccurate description in an otherwise carefully wrought story. It also needs to be noted that Mr. B. cannot have an idea that the apparition will turn out to be his own daughter; another moment of gothic anticipation, however, becomes visible at this point in that the girl "expressed filial affection, and asked parental pity."

Scattered throughout the text are a number of additional terms and expressions that add to the gothic nature of the text: "something more than human," "deadly pallidness," "angel in distress," "supernatural," "inexplicable enigma," and "vision," among others. All of these create what Freud calls "das Unheimliche," the uncanny, the very core of gothic tales.[9]

The background of the gothic motifs in "Something Unaccountable" is identifiable as Euro-American folk culture. Listed alphabetically by their index numbers, the following motifs can clearly be made out:

> Revenant in a female dress (E 422.2.4)
> Appearance of ghost serves as death omen. Often the appearance is not recognized as a death omen until the death is reported by other means (E 574)[10]

Whether or not E 545.3, *Dead announces its own death*, is also present, is arguable since there is no such thing as an actual announcement on the part of the apparition. Depending on the interpretation of various parts of the story, some additional ones can be added:

Magic power of children (D 1717)
Misfortune from mistaken interpretation of prophecy (N 398)
Death of children as punishment (Q 553.4)

As mentioned above, whether or not one accepts the presence of these motifs in the text depends on the various possible interpretations of certain segments of the story. Depending on the nature and cause of the apparition, little Amelia might have magic powers. If a moral reading is preferred, and the description of the apparition really shows sexual attraction, then—but only then—can her death appear as punishment. The whole incident might just as well be interpreted as a prophecy designed to distract Mr. B. from falling in love with his future wife, making it a prophecy misunderstood.

There is at least one more motif which is rather prominent, but its reading once again depends on how one interprets the story: F575.3, a *Remarkably Beautiful Child*. Though not mentioned by Thompson, taking this motif to its extreme creates the notion of an *Angelic Child*. This reading excludes a sexual connotation, and given traditional folktale conventions as well as reader preferences in the late 1700s, the readers of *The Massachusetts Magazine* are likely to have identified this motif from the text. With her ethereal beauty and perfection, Amelia's apparition looks better and larger than life, a motif repeated in the text when she enters the Academy for young ladies, and the writer is introduced to her. The symbolism connected to this motif can be summarized as "beautiful children do not last," which is exactly what happens here.

What is so interesting about all these motifs is how the author actually connects and blends them. The apparition itself features three to four of them, depending on varying interpretations. Following British folk conventions, this would have been highly unlikely. By mixing different already existing motifs and creating something new, Z. P. departed from the well-trodden paths. While a reading assigning a nationalist agency to the author at this point would be in all likelihood an exaggeration, the open form of the story still shows a certain degree of formal experimentalism coinciding with an initial deviation of American literature from British traditions.

Perceiving of the collection of stories in this volume as a document of a development of a new genre striving to find its form and gradually establishing new reading and writing conventions, "Something Unaccountable" can be read as a missing link between the earliest short stories and the works of Poe and Hawthorne. Its extreme openness to multiple interpretations, and its design of a unity of effect without any apparent moral, make a case for a classification as an early American short story. "Something Unaccountable" features all major aspects described in Poe's review of Hawthorne's *Twice-Told Tales*.[11] Attentive readers will recognize the half-hidden indications leading to the calamitous ending.

But if the ending comes as a surprise, there is even more reason for readers to re-examine the story, looking for a missed clue as to why this girl had to die. Not finding any but led to explore multiple possible interpretations, the reader might then identify hints unnoticed during the first reading, but will see that there are motifs and details he or she is still not able to assign a clear meaning to. There is no one moral message. "Something Unaccountable" is more than yet another early American literary attempt at short prose fiction. This is indeed, as Jack B. Moore claimed, a "neglected early American Short Story."[12]

Aynur Erdogan, Philipp Fidler

Notes

[1] Jack B. Moore, "A Neglected Early American Short Story," *American Notes and Queries* 4 (1966): 84–86.

[2] Edward W. R. Pitcher, ed., *An Anthology of the Short Story in 18th and 19th Century America*, 2 vols. (Lewiston: Edwin Mellen P, 2000) 2: 471–74.

[3] Caravansary is a roadside inn for travelers.

[4] Preceptress is a headmistress or female head teacher.

[5] Putrid fever is typhoid fever, caused by louse-borne bacteria.

[6] Note the analogy to Christ's speech before his crucifixion: "Not my will, but thine, be done" (Luke 22:42).

[7] Daniel J. Boorstin, *The Genius of American Politics* (Chicago: U of Chicago P, 1956): 46.

[8] Cf. David Mogen et al., Introduction, *Frontier Gothic: Terror and Wonder at the Frontier in American Literature*, eds. David Mogen, Scott P. Sanders, and Joanne B. Karpinski (Rutherford: Farleigh Dickinson UP, 1993): 15.

[9] Allan Lloyd-Smith, *American Gothic Fiction* (New York: Continuum, 2004): 74–75.

[10] All index numbers refer to Stith Thompson, *Motif-Index of Folk-Literature: A Classification of Narrative Elements in Folktales, Ballads, Myths, Fables, Mediaeval Romances, Exempla,*

Fabliaux, Jest-Books and Local Legends, 6 vols. (Bloomington: Indiana UP, 1989).

[11] Edgar A. Poe, "Nathaniel Hawthorne: Twice-Told Tales," *The Complete Works of Edgar Allan Poe,* ed. James A. Harrison, 17 vols. (New York: AMS P, 1979) 11: 108.

[12] Moore, "A Neglected Early American Short Story," 84.

Narrative of the Unpardonable Sin

N.

Whether or not the "Narrative of the Unpardonable Sin" was intended to be read as fictional short prose is doubtful, given its original place of publication: It first appeared in Cornelius Davis' New York periodical The Theological Magazine, or Synopsis of Modern Religious Sentiment *in 1797. Although N., the author of the text, has not been identified, no other contemporary publication of this text is known, which strongly suggests that it is an original American magazine contribution.*

The thematic issue of the "Unpardonable Sin" also strongly suggests an American origin. In the story, a theological discussion is exemplified in narrative form: A young man, in both his physical and mental condition, represents a generic sinner who has committed the one sin against the Holy Ghost which, according to the Bible, is unpardonable. Because the unpardonable sin is found in the Gospels according to Matthew, Mark, and Luke, apparently no further explication was deemed necessary, nor is there a didactic moral at the end of the story.

This textual configuration, and the sentiments that the story expresses, make the "Unpardonable Sin" a forerunner of certain 19th century short stories. Edward W. R. Pitcher points out that later "narratives of characters with tormented consciences (those guilty of an unpardonable sin) *are direct descendents."[1] One only needs to think of Nathaniel Hawthorne's "Ethan Brand" to see the similarities.*

On the contemporary level, the "Narrative of the Unpardonable Sin" is more directly related to religious discussions of the period. The protagonist's experiences of the effects of his exceptional sin parallel the doctrines of evangelists of the Great Awakening in America. In this sense, the theme of the story is embedded in the specific context of American Puritanism.

Narrative of the Unpardonable Sin[2]

Mr. Editor,
If you judge the following Narrative merits a Place in your Magazine, please to insert it.

But a few years since, in my travels, I was invited to preach a lecture in a town, where the work of God, in awakening, convincing, and changing the hearts of sinners prevailed.[3] After the lecture I conversed with a number of persons about the great concerns of their souls. Directly one of the assembly came to me, and informed me of a certain young man, who said he had committed the unpardonable sin, and desired me to converse with him. He was accordingly brought forward. After asking him a few questions, to ascertain, in some measure, his feelings, I endeavoured to convince him, that he was under peculiar temptation, and had no reason to despair of mercy: for at that time I did not suppose his apprehensions respecting himself were well founded. "It is in vain," said he, "to labour with me in this manner, for I *know* I have committed that sin against the Holy Ghost, which is unpardonable, and never, never, can mercy be exercised towards me."

These words were spoken with such emphasis, and his countenance at the same time discovered something so very uncommon, that they made a strong impression on my mind, and produced in me a desire to be more particular in my inquiries. I asked him if he knew when he committed that sin, and what made him believe it was the unpardonable sin? He then gave this account. "He had been, he said, under religious impressions for some time, till, at last, he was beset with a strong temptation to do a certain thing, which he knew was expressly prohibited in the word of God. What it was he was tempted to do he would not tell. He resisted, he said, the temptation for some time—reflected upon the subject frequently, whether he could entertain any hope of salvation, if he should commit that sin. At last, he said, within himself, 'I will do the thing if I am damned forever the next hour,' and accordingly did it. Immediately, said he, I had feelings which I never experienced in such a sensible degree before—his heart became hard as an adamant—his enmity against God increased to a great degree. Since that time he had not felt one desire to ask or receive mercy, or the least favour of God. He never reflected on the divine character, but his heart rose in the most violent opposition. Whenever, said he, I reflect that God is Almighty, just, and holy—that I am dependent on him—that he can and will do with me as he pleases, my heart burns with rage and fury, and had I power, I would execute vengeance on the Almighty."[4]

He then addressed himself to a number under religious impressions who stood around. "I have heard you relate the feelings of your hearts, and you appear to have some sense of your wickedness; but if enmity of heart against God is wickedness, (and that it is, I am fully convinced, though I wish to believe to the contrary) your present sense is nothing compared with the fountain of iniquity within. I know, if all men's hearts are naturally alike, you would dethrone the Almighty if you had power. Had I an omnipotent arm, heaven would soon be stormed, and God be cast headlong from this throne." In expressions like these, he uttered himself for some time, to appearance actuated with the highest rage. "I have no peace, said he, day nor night, my torment is as great, seemingly, as I can endure. God is constantly in my view, and my heart is constantly burning with rage and fury." His eyes, his countenance and air, expressed the same feelings with his words; such a sight I never saw since nor before. Nothing I could say availed any thing, unless to increase his rage and enmity. He had, as it appeared to me, the most clear and lively sense of the wickedness of the human heart—of the divine character—the creature's dependence, and the nature of future torments of any person with whom I was ever acquainted.

Some of his friends told me, that his distress was sometimes so great, that he would lie down and roll on the floor from one side of the room to the other, and groan like a man exercised with excruciating pain, and cry, Oh! that I could banish all thoughts of God from my mind forever and ever. At one time he travelled barefoot in the night, twelve miles, in a deep snow, without making one stop. He was followed by the track he made, and when enquired of, why he conducted thus, he replied, "that bodily pain was the only mean by which he could divert his mind from those objects which gave him greater distress than what he experienced in his travel. He, therefore, did it to mitigate his distress." This person exhibited to my view a lively picture of hell, where the anguish and distress of all impenitent sinners will exceed all expression, when they have a lively sense of divine and eternal realities.

Critical Commentary

The *Theological Magazine, or Synopsis of Modern Religious Sentiment*, where the "Narrative of the Unpardonable Sin" first appeared, was edited and published by Cornelius Davis from July 1795 to February 1799. This time span puts the publication of the magazine in what Frank L. Mott called the "Period of Nationalism" following the Postal Act of 1794.[5] This period proved to be prolific "in the founding of religious magazines and in religious discussions in secular periodicals."[6] Although, as Mott points out, religious topics were an integral part of magazines before, only five religious magazines existed in the previous period (1741–1794).[7] However, the end of the 18th century and the first quarter of the 19th century saw a dramatic rise of religious periodicals. Notably the First Amendment to the Constitution, but also the increasing number of immigrants, brought about "a situation in which new innovative religious gestalts could emerge."[8]

While some religious periodicals were addressed to a specific denomination, others dealt with general religious topics and themes. It is the latter category that the *Theological Magazine* falls into. In a time when rationalism was gaining influence, Davis announced in his first editorial that the aim of his magazine was to provide "a vehicle for religious knowledge and candid disquisition, and afford the friends of truth and rational inquiry, an opportunity to publish their opinions, queries, and arguments, and submit them to the scrutiny of the wise and judicious." Based on "a design so liberal and well adapted to promote a spirit of free inquiry," it was conceived to convey "a variety of useful information, concerning the doctrines and practice of religion."[9] The following year, Davis openly encouraged "the serious and judicious of all denominations" to contribute articles that were "useful and entertaining."[10]

The "Narrative of the Unpardonable Sin" was apparently one of the texts sent to Davis after this call for submissions. Although Jack B. Moore deduces from other writings in the magazine that the author, N., "appears to be a Vermont clergyman," this can only be considered speculation.[11] There are several other articles in the *Theological Magazine* attributed to "N.," but they do not include any information on location, nor do they bear any significant resemblance in style, form or content to the "Narrative of the Unpardonable Sin."[12]

In order to address the American origin and literary characteristics of the "Narrative of the Unpardonable Sin," an understanding of its theological context needs to be highlighted. It can be shown that many of the motifs, and even individual phrasings, in the "Unpardonable Sin" correspond to the Puritan theology of the evangelical revival, particularly to the preaching and writings of Jonathan Edwards who led the discussion on the existence and form of the unpardonable sin.

As its title and place of publication indicate, the "Narrative of the Unpardonable Sin" is a theological discussion of the one sin that cannot be forgiven: blasphemy of the Holy Ghost (or Spirit of God). There are three references to such a sin in the New Testament: Matthew 12:31–32, Mark 3:28–30, and Luke 12:8–10. In all three descriptions, blasphemy of the Holy Ghost is presented as the one unpardonable sin. The concept of blasphemy has been discussed among theologians throughout the centuries, and according to Jonathan Edwards, there are three things essential to the unpardonable sin—and all three are meticulously included in the story as constitutive parts of the mental condition of the young man: conviction, malice, and presumption. With respect to the first element Edwards states that for a man to blaspheme the Holy Ghost, his action "must be attended with conviction; he must be sensible that he does it; he must be sensible that the thing he reviles is God's Spirit."[13]

The story also uses Edwards' terms to describe the actual commitment of the sin and its results. In other words, the influence of the writings of Jonathan Edwards is evident all through the text, though some notions are traceable to earlier American Puritans. Thomas Hooker, for example, preceded Edwards in pointing out the readiness of sinners to overthrow God: "Now herein lies the inconceivable heinousness of the hellish nature of sin: it would jostle the Almighty out of the throne of His glorious sovereignty, and indeed be above Him."[14] However, Edwards reserves the attempt to overthrow God to those who commit the unpardonable sin.

One further indication of the indebtedness of N.'s story to Edwards is the fact that the heart of the sinner is described as becoming hard and adamant: In the biblical sense, the heart rarely represents the physical organ but is used as a metaphor for the center of the individual's spiritual, intellectual, and emotional life. With respect to an evangelical awakening, it is the heart that plays a central role in the awakening or revival process.

Although an awakening or conversion can elevate man from his state of sin and thereby save him from condemnation and God's wrath, Edwards, in his sermon "Sinners in the Hands of an Angry God," states that those who

THE UNPARDONABLE SIN 161

> never passed under a great change of heart, by the mighty power of the Spirit of God . . . that were never born again, and made new creatures, and raised from being dead in sin, to a state of new, and before altogether unexperienced light and life . . . are thus in the hands of an angry God.[15]

These sinners, however, will not only experience God's wrath on Judgment Day, they will also experience it during their worldly and unregenerate life. This is exactly what happens to the young man in the story.

Looking at the "Narrative of the Unpardonable Sin" and keeping the doctrine of sin of the evangelical revival in mind, it is quite obvious that the depiction of the young man's sin and its effects on him mirror the features of sin and its effects on the sinner as presented in Edwards' sermons. In the story, the sinner is not in a natural condition of ignorance. Yet, while being convinced of one's sinfulness is according to Edwards the prerequisite for the conversion to God, the sinner's heart in the story is petrified: He has not committed just any sin but willingly "that sin against the Holy Ghost, which is unpardonable." It is the nature of the willfully committed sin that makes a conversion impossible and leads to irrecoverable hardening of the heart.

The young man in the text is full of anger and, parallel to Edwards' statement about the effects of the perverse disposition of the sinner's heart, he feels the desire to dethrone God. Even further in line with Edwards' depiction of the unpardonable sin, the young man also presents his enmity toward God publicly. At the same time, he experiences torments and distress which cannot be mitigated due to the severity of his sin. According to Edwards' doctrine of sin, the sinner's distress is the result, not of his feeling of guilt, but of his being no longer "held in the hand of God, over the pit of hell."[16] The irrecoverable sinner already experiences hell itself.

The parallels between the young man's unpardonable sin and the doctrines of Jonathan Edwards and the Great Awakening clearly place the story in an American cultural context. At the same time, the use of two established text types, the exemplum and the moral tale, contribute to the form of the "Narrative of the Unpardonable Sin." The exemplum and the moral tale are clearly linked to the theological argumentation of the story, but the narrative form of the story is not limited to either of them. Instead, the story integrates elements borrowed from both the exemplum and the moral tale, resulting in a textual formation that can be identified as an emerging short story.

Traditionally in American culture, the exemplum is part of a sermon which provides the frame, based on a theoretical question that is biblical in origin. The exemplum transports the religious problem onto the level of the audience's everyday experience. What makes the "Unpardonable Sin" unusual is that the theoretical frame is integrated into the narrative: The articulation of an abstract theological problem into an everyday encounter serves to concretize the story, while the extraordinary case of the young man places the encounter within the short story format.

Even if the moral is the main purpose of the text, as far as its intentionality is concerned, there are moments pointing to other potential readings. For example, the sinner's rhetoric mirrors and even copies Puritan rhetoric, and although he is not a developed character, his direct confrontation with the minister, plus the use of direct speech, creates the notion of an actual person: His experience is related as if it really happened. This sense of the young man's presence in the text allows for a reading that overcomes the didactic distance of the typical exemplum format. The effects of committing the unpardonable sin are still illustrated and commented upon, of course, but the classical frame of the exemplum is missing. The illustration is interspersed with the narrator's comments, thereby integrating into the story the explanation of the events, an element that traditionally follows the exemplum. As a result, the narrative form of the exemplum, which is still obvious in such texts as "The Story of the Captain's Wife and an Aged Woman," is here transformed into a proto-short story.

Similarly, the story's use of the moral tale also diverges from the format in which it is found in such texts as the "Story of Julia." While the "Unpardonable Sin" does not contain overt didacticism in the sense of explicitly giving advice with respect to moral behavior, it contains an illustration of the theological doctrine of the unpardonable sin. Thus, the text does contain what Pitcher describes as the "subjugation of fiction to an unwritten code of socio-moral utilitarianism."[17] To the extent that there is intrusive authorial commentary, illustration of a moral thesis, and the use of the familiar (the Bible, and the preaching of Jonathan Edwards), the literary characteristics of the story place it in the distinctly 18th century form of the moral tale.

Moral tales inherently attempt to teach a lesson. According to Pitcher, they attempt to deter the reader "from vice or folly, and to excite him to emulate and practice virtue."[18] Pitcher goes on to say that moralists "wished to create the illusion that the tale was the record of a real individual's experience in the contemporary world," but in order to make the story's moral message applicable to a diverse audience, they emphasized that the "individual's life had to be representative, and the patterns of cause and effect within it had to be typical."[19] The analogies between what Pitcher defines as the moral tale and the "Narrative of the Unpardonable Sin" are evident. However, several elements of the text, while not exactly standing in opposition to the features of the moral tale, anticipate another literary format.

It is true that the characters—the narrator, the young man, and the friends—are not developed in the sense that they are individualized by names or that they undergo any discernible development. Also, there is no background information about them, so that they appear as generic types in this respect. And the narrator, although identified as a minister, is otherwise a generic figure. However, the lack of the sermonic frame in the text creates an immediate rendition of the dramatic confrontation between an irredeemable sinner and a minister who is, after all, powerless in his presence—not usually the position ministers like to find themselves in. Even if this sinner is not an Ethan Brand, neither is he a mere allegory. In addition, the narrative nature of the text makes it impossible for any moral message beyond a somewhat helpless warning not to commit the unpardonable sin.

The combination of features of several divergent literary forms results in the "Narrative of the Unpardonable Sin" conforming to none. The coalition of different types of fictional prose in the text along with employing a variety of different narrative strategies is of singular significance for the literary quality of the text. And the convergence of forms and techniques, and the ensuing paradigm shift from moral purpose to unity of effect, are fundamental aspects with respect to the creation of the literary form of the early short story.

The story is developed around the theme of the unpardonable sin and it focuses on the illustration of the effects of the sin on the sinner. Yet it depicts a momentous situation that strongly unifies the text and emphasizes its effect. The unity of the text is also sustained by a strict economy of means, such as a focus on the sinner's predicament. As a result, the text achieves its "calculated brevity."[20]

There is yet another aspect to determining whether the text can indeed be categorized as an early short story. The "Narrative of the Unpardonable Sin" undeniably contains didacticism, and the narrator's comments are intended to provide the reader with moral guidance, but neither of these aspects manages to deprive the text of its structural ambiguity. The use of literary strategies such as a frame narrative and dialogue, although not applied in a very refined manner, point to a concern with literary aestheticism and, to a certain extent, with entertainment. It is not a full-fledged short story yet, but its dramatic focus on a Puritan nightmare anticipates later stories, notably those of Nathaniel Hawthorne.

Anita Schneider

Notes

[1] Edward W. R. Pitcher, Introduction, *An Anthology of the Short Story in 18th and 19th Century America,* ed. Edward W. R. Pitcher, 2 vols. (Lewiston: Edwin Mellen P, 2000) 1: 32.

[2] There is no title to the story in the magazine itself; in the table of contents it is listed as "Sin, Narrative of the Unpardonable." Pitcher reprinted it in his *Anthology* with the current title.

[3] The choice of words (awakening, convincing, and changing the hearts of sinners) alludes to the aim of evangelical awakening, namely, the conversion of individuals from a state of sin to a rebirth, as pursued by the Puritan preachers Jonathan Edwards and George Whitefield throughout the period of the Great Awakening (1730–1760).

[4] In the Bible, fury is often paralleled with the words anger and wrath. The Hebrew origin of the word fury, *hema*, literally means heat or burning.

[5] Frank Luther Mott, *A History of American Magazine:, 1741–1850* (Cambridge, MA: Harvard UP, 1957): 94.

[6] Mott, *A History of American Magazines* 131.

[7] Mott, *A History of American Magazines* 56.

[8] Gordon Melton, *The Encyclopedia of American Religions* (Detroit: Gale Research, 1989): 8.

[9] Cornelius Davis, "Introduction," *The Theological Magazine* 1 (1795): 3, 5.

[10] Cornelius Davis, "Preface," *The Theological Magazine* 1 (1796): 3.

[11] Jack B. Moore, "The First 'Narrative of the Unpardonable Sin,'" *Discourse* 10 (1967): 278.

[12] The texts are mainly essays or theoretical discussions, for example, "Remarks on the History of Haman," "Consequences of Universal Salvation," and "On the Love of our Neighbour".

[13] Jonathan Edwards, *The "Miscellanies,"* ed. Thomas A. Schafer (New Haven: Yale UP, 1994) Vol. 13 of *The Works of Jonathan Edwards,* 26 vols. 517–18.

[14] Thomas Hooker, "A True Sight of Sin," *The American Puritans: Their Prose and Poetry,* ed., Perry Miller (New York: Columbia UP: 1956): 155.

[15] Jonathan Edwards, "Sermons and Discourses: 1739–1742," ed. Harry S. Stout (New Haven: Yale UP, 2003) Vol. 22 of *The Works of Jonathan Edwards,* 26 vols. 411.

[16] Edwards, "Sermons and Discourses: 1739–1742" 409.

[17] Pitcher, "Introduction" 3.
[18] Pitcher, "Introduction" 6.
[19] Pitcher, "Introduction" 10.
[20] Barbara Korte, *The Short Story in Britain* (Tübingen: Francke UTB, 2003): 5.

The Adventure of the German Student
Washington Irving

"The Adventure of the German Student" was printed first in the "Strange Stories by a Nervous Gentleman" section of Washington Irving's Tales of a Traveller *in 1824. It has since been included in a variety of anthologies. In all of these anthologized versions, the lines linking the "German Student" to the preceding story in* Tales of a Traveller *are omitted. This story of "The Bold Dragoon," narrated by his grandson, a captain in the Irish dragoons, ends with an old gentleman with a "haunted head" assuming the role of the narrator. Up to this point, all of the stories told have remained somehow unfinished (and therefore impossible to anthologize). Now the gentleman with the haunted head announces: "I recollect an adventure, however . . . which I heard of during a residence at Paris, for the truth of which I can undertake to vouch, and which is of a very grave and singular nature."[1] This creates a full frame for the story which otherwise ends somewhat unexpectedly with the metanarrative comments by the "gentleman with the haunted head" and the "inquisitive gentleman," both of whom are members of a circle of travelers accidentally thrown together at a fox-hunting event.*

This narrative frame echoes and continues the British periodical essay, which Irving of course was familiar with. Its ancestral roots go back even further, to the story cycles of Boccaccio and Chaucer, who used the narrative frame as a linking device between thematically related tales. The "German Student" therefore deviates from the rest of the stories in this collection in that its background does not include magazine publication. It deviates further in that we know its author, and even further if we consider that Irving wrote the collection with both eyes on the European market, where he lived, and where his work met with considerable success. If there is anything in the story itself that would make the text appear American—for the setting and the characters are evidently European—it is the implicit and ironic critique of the revolutionary fervor shaking old Europe, and potentially shaking the roots of the democratic form of capitalism that had established itself in the U.S.[2]

The reason we include "The Adventure of the German Student" here is that it conforms, in all aspects of form and narrative technique, to the genre that Edgar Allan Poe in his review of Hawthorne's Twice-Told Tales was to call, twenty years later, the "tale proper." Poe's "tale proper" in turn paved the way for what is known today as the American short story.

The Adventure of the German Student

In a stormy night, in the tempestuous times of the French Revolution, a young German was returning to his lodgings, at a late hour, across the old part of Paris. The lightning gleamed, and the loud claps of thunder rattled through the lofty narrow streets—but I should first tell you something about this young German.

Gottfried Wolfgang was a young man of good family. He had studied for some time at Göttingen, but being of a visionary and enthusiastic character, he had wandered into those wild and speculative doctrines which have so often bewildered German students.[3] His secluded life, his intense application, and the singular nature of his studies, had an effect on both mind and body. His health was impaired; his imagination diseased. He had been indulging in fanciful speculations on spiritual essences, until, like Swedenborg, he had an ideal world of his own around him.[4] He took up a notion, I do not know from what cause, that there was an evil influence hanging over him; an evil genius or spirit seeking to ensnare him and ensure his perdition. Such an idea working on his melancholy temperament produced the most gloomy effects. He became haggard and desponding. His friends discovered the mental malady preying upon him, and determined that the best cure was a change of scene; he was sent, therefore, to finish his studies amidst the splendors and gayeties of Paris.

Wolfgang arrived at Paris at the breaking out of the revolution. The popular delirium at first caught his enthusiastic mind, and he was captivated by the political and philosophical theories of the day: but the scenes of blood which followed shocked his sensitive nature, disgusted him with society and the world, and made him more than ever a recluse.[5] He shut himself up in a solitary apartment in the *Pays Latin,* the quarter of students. There, in a gloomy street not far from the monastic walls of the Sorbonne, he pursued his favorite speculations.[6] Sometimes he spent hours in the great libraries of Paris, those catacombs of departed authors, rummaging among their hoards of dusty and obsolete works in quest of food for his unhealthy appetite. He was, in a manner, a literary ghoul, feeding in the charnel-house of decayed literature.

Wolfgang, though solitary and recluse, was of an ardent temperament, but for a time it operated merely upon his imagination. He was too shy and ignorant of the world to make any advances to the fair, but he was a passionate admirer of female beauty, and in his lonely chamber would often lose himself in reveries on forms and faces which he had seen, and his fancy would deck out images of loveliness far surpassing the reality.

While his mind was in this excited and sublimated state, a dream produced an extraordinary effect upon him. It was of a female face of transcendent beauty. So strong was the impression made, that he dreamt of it again and again. It haunted his thoughts by day, his slumbers by night; in fine, he became passionately enamored of this shadow of a dream. This lasted so long that it became one of those fixed ideas which haunt the minds of melancholy men, and are at times mistaken for madness.

Such was Gottfried Wolfgang, and such his situation at the time I mentioned. He was returning home late on stormy night, through some of the old and gloomy streets of the *Marais,* the ancient part of Paris. The loud claps of thunder rattled among the high houses of the narrow streets. He came to the Place de Grève, the square where public executions are performed. The lightning quivered about the pinnacles of the ancient Hôtel de Ville, and shed flickering gleams over the open space in front.[7] As Wolfgang was crossing the square, he shrank back with horror at finding himself close by the guillotine. It was the height of the reign of terror, when this dreadful instrument of death stood ever ready, and its scaffold was continually running with the blood of the virtuous and the brave. It had that very day been actively employed in the work of carnage, and there it stood in grim array, amidst a silent and sleeping city, waiting for fresh victims.

Wolfgang's heart sickened within him, and he was turning shuddering from the horrible engine, when he beheld a shadowy form, cowering as it were at the foot of the steps which led up to the scaffold. A succession of vivid flashes of lightning revealed it more distinctly. It was a female figure, dressed in black. She was seated on one of the lower steps of the scaffold, leaning forward, her face hid in her lap; and her long disheveled tresses hanging to the ground, streaming with the rain which fell in torrents. Wolfgang paused. There was something awful in this solitary monument of woe. The female had the appearance of being above the common order. He knew the times to be full of vicissitude, and that many a fair head, which had once been pillowed on down, now wandered houseless. Perhaps this was some poor mourner whom the dreadful axe had rendered desolate, and who sat here heart-broken on the strand of existence, from which all that was dear to her had been launched into eternity.

He approached, and addressed her in the accents of sympathy. She raised her head and gazed wildly at him. What was his astonishment at beholding, by the bright glare of the lighting, the very face which had haunted him in his dreams. It was pale and disconsolate, but ravishingly beautiful.

Trembling with violent and conflicting emotions, Wolfgang again accosted her. He spoke something of her being exposed at such an hour of the night, and to the fury of such a storm, and offered to conduct her to her friends. She pointed to the guillotine with a gesture of dreadful signification.

"I have no friend on earth!" said she.

"But you have a home," said Wolfgang.

"Yes—in the grave!"

The heart of the student melted at the words.

"If a stranger dare make an offer," said he, "without danger of being misunderstood, I would offer my humble dwelling as a shelter; myself as a devoted friend. I am friendless myself in Paris, and a stranger in the land; but if my life could be of service, it is at your disposal, and should be sacrificed before harm or indignity should come to you."

There was an honest earnestness in the young man's manner that had its effect. His foreign accent, too, was in his favour; it showed him not to be a hackneyed inhabitant of Paris. Indeed, there is an eloquence in true enthusiasm that is not to be doubted. The homeless stranger confided herself implicitly to the protection of the student.

He supported her faltering steps across the Pont Neuf, and by the place where the statue of Henry the Fourth had been overthrown by the populace. The storm had abated, and the thunder rumbled at a distance. All Paris was quiet; that great volcano of human passion slumbered for a while, to gather fresh strength for the next day's eruption. The student conducted his charge through the ancient streets of the *Pays Latin,* and by the dusky walls of the Sorbonne, to the great dingy hotel which he inhabited. The old porteress who admitted them stared with surprise at the unusual sight of the melancholy Wolfgang, with a female companion.

On entering his apartment, the student, for the first time, blushed at the scantiness and indifference of his dwelling. He had but one chamber—an old-fashioned saloon—heavily carved, and fantastically furnished with the remains of former magnificence, for it was one of those hotels in the quarter of the Luxembourg palace, which had once belonged to nobility. It was lumbered with books and papers, and all the usual apparatus of a student, and his bed stood in a recess at one end.

When lights were brought, and Wolfgang had a better opportunity of contemplating the stranger, he was more than ever intoxicated by her beauty. Her face was pale, but of a dazzling fairness, set off by a profusion of raven hair that hung clustering about it. Her eyes were large and brilliant, with a singular expression approaching almost to wildness. As far as her black dress permitted her shape to be seen, it was of perfect symmetry. Her whole appearance was highly striking, though she was dressed in the simplest style. The only thing approaching to an ornament which she wore, was a broad black band round her neck, clasped by diamonds.

The perplexity now commenced with the student how to dispose of the helpless being thus thrown upon his protection. He thought of abandoning his chamber to her, and seeking shelter for himself elsewhere. Still, he was so fascinated by her charms, there seemed to be such a spell upon his thoughts and senses, that he could not tear himself from her presence. Her manner, too, was singular and unaccountable. She spoke no more of the guillotine. Her grief had abated. The attentions of the student had first won her confidence, and then, apparently, her heart. She was evidently an enthusiast like himself, and enthusiasts soon understand each other.

In the infatuation of the moment, Wolfgang avowed his passion for her. He told her the story of his mysterious dream, and how she had possessed his heart before he had even seen her. She was strangely affected by his recital, and acknowledged to have felt an impulse toward him equally unaccountable. It was the time for wild theory and wild actions. Old prejudices and superstitions were done away; everything was under the sway of the "Goddess of Reason." Among other rubbish of the old times, the forms and ceremonies of marriage began to be considered superfluous bonds for honorable minds. Social compacts were the vogue. Wolfgang was too much of theorist not to be tainted by the liberal doctrines of the day.

"Why should we separate?" said he: "our hearts are united; in the eye of reason and honor we are as one. What need is there of sordid forms to bind high souls together?"

The stranger listened with emotion: she had evidently received illumination at the same school.

"You have no home nor family," continued he: "let me be everything to you, or rather let us be everything to one another. If form is necessary, form shall be observed—there is my hand. I pledge myself to you forever."

"Forever?" said the stranger, solemnly.

"Forever!" repeated Wolfgang.

The stranger clasped the hand extended to her: "Then I am yours," murmured she, and sank upon his bosom.

The next morning the student left his bride sleeping, and sallied forth at an early hour to seek more spacious apartments suitable to the change in his situation. When he returned, he found the stranger lying with her head hanging over the bed, and one arm thrown over it. He spoke to her, but received no reply. He advanced to awaken her from her uneasy posture. On taking her hand, it was cold—there was no pulsation—her face was pallid and ghastly. In a word, she was a corpse.

Horrified and frantic, he alarmed the house. A scene of confusion ensued. The police was summoned. As the officer of police entered the room, he started back on beholding the corpse.

"Great heaven!" cried he, "how did this woman come here?"

"Do you know anything about her?" said Wolfgang eagerly.

"Do I?" exclaimed the officer: "she was guillotined yesterday."

He stepped forward; undid the black collar round the neck of the corpse, and the head rolled on the floor!

The student burst into a frenzy. "The fiend! the fiend has gained possession of me!" shrieked he; "I am lost forever."

They tried to soothe him, but in vain. He was possessed with the frightful belief that an evil spirit had reanimated the dead body to ensnare him. He went distracted, and died in a mad-house.

Here the old gentleman with the haunted head finished his narrative.

"And is this really a fact?" said the inquisitive gentleman.

"A fact not to be doubted," replied the other. "I had it from the best authority. The student told it me himself. I saw him in a mad-house in Paris."

Critical Commentary

While there can be no doubt that the story makes use of Gothic elements, and of a somewhat awkward sleight-of-hand trick to bring about narrative closure, this story is in several ways more important within the context of the history of the early American short story than has so far been acknowledged. For one, it is a brilliant parody of Gothic fiction, which was already being played out in Washington Irving's time. Secondly, it simultaneously asserted the continuing power of the genre to shock through sudden revelations and psychological depth.[8] But even more important is the position that "The Adventure of the German Student" holds in American literary history. Even though "Rip van Winkle" and "The Legend of Sleepy Hollow"—perhaps because of their overt Americanness—are usually cited as the first American short stories, they fail to fulfill the potential of the genre. Instead, it is "The Adventure of the German Student" that is one of the first fully formed short stories, anticipating the initial heyday of American short story writing as exemplified in the works of Edgar Allan Poe, Nathaniel Hawthorne, and Herman Melville.

In contrast to the far more loosely constructed stories of Rip van Winkle and Ichabod Crane, the "German Student" clearly adheres to the principle of calculated brevity so essential in the formation of the short story: With the exception of a brief narrative review of Gottfried Wolfgang's stereotypical Göttingen University background, the setting is within the old town of Paris; the time span, after telescoping three years into one line, is limited to one night and the following morning. There is no elaborate plot: The student, returning home, finds the disconsolate woman he has been dreaming about on the steps leading up to the guillotine, takes her home, and finds her dead the next morning. Most of the dialogue takes place between these two figures, of which only the student is characterized to some degree. Of the woman, the reader learns no more than that she is strikingly beautiful and apparently willing to assent in becoming the student's common law wife. She remains, quite literally, shadowy, in the tradition of a female gothic figure, a figure Poe categorized when he quipped that the most poetic topic was the death of a beautiful woman.

The relation between Irving's "German Student" and the gothic genre as it appeared in British and American magazines of the time—the latter often pirated reprints of the former—parallels the similarities that Simone Hagenmeyer found in comparing Irving's essays in *Oldschool* and *Salmagundi* to their counterparts in British periodicals.[9] The difference is usually gradual and often satirical or ironic: The ancestral form remains recognizable and can still be read as such if the reader insists on it; the new—American—reader, however, will see the irony and with it the subversion.

Irving himself stated his aim in the foreword to *Bracebridge Hall* with almost classical understatement: "In venturing occasionally on topics that have already been almost exhausted by English authors, I do it, not with the presumption of challenging a comparison, but with the hope that some new interest may be given to such topics, when discussed by the pen of a stranger."[10]

In "The Adventure of the German Student," this doubling takes on the form of almost physically graspable irony. While on one level the student appears as the traditional haunted figure with an obsessed challenged mind, and the setting as well as the events conform to gothic forebears, there is a second, and even a third level of meaning. On the second level, what John Glendenning called "an inverted gothic" comes to play.[11] Besides the gothic ghost story, Irving leaves the possibility that the diseased imagination of the student makes him a ghoul who carries home a corpse to have intercourse with, believing that she is the woman of his dreams and turning to necrophilia when he finds her dead.[12] Barbara Tepa Lupack adds a third reading, in which the woman is a mere figment of the student's imagination, an imagination that we learn early on is "diseased."[13] This interpretation, however, only holds if the whole event is a madman's narrative, since within the story characters other than the student also see the beautiful woman dead on his bed. On this level, however, there are again two possibilities: The "gentleman with the haunted head" is relating a true story of an unfortunate German student he once met in a Paris madhouse, or the whole story is a hoax, where the preceding story disintegrates with the revelation of its source. This in turn would make the "German Student" an early example of what has been claimed as a typical American format, the dead-pan narration. Thus there are two doublings, or ambiguous alternatives, that open up to traditional gothic readings, or their comical inversions. This doubling as an issue in the story is supported by the very name of the main character: As Barbara Tepa Lupack has pointed out, "Gottfried" literally means "in God's peace," which is clearly not the condition the student finds himself in.[14] What Lupack fails to mention, however, is the student's first name: Wolfgang—one who runs with the wolves. With this in mind, the fact that he has *"wandered into* those wild and speculative doctrines which have so often bewildered German students," takes on the ironic quality and implicit double meaning that many of Irving's little rhetorical twists and turns can lay claim to, such as when the woman says her home is "in the grave."

It is clearly visible that the story answers to the principle of unity of effect in so far as the ultimate ambiguity is conscientiously built up throughout the story in a series of rhetorical *double entendres*, leaving traces of ambivalence from the very beginning. That is, it leaves these traces for attentive readers. Like so many of Poe's, and later on, of Melville's stories, "The Adventure of the German Student" is not meant to be read but reread: Poe's theory, as well as his own practice, calls for an attentive reader whose multiple readings lift the short story above the level of light reading that is perused in a half-distracted mode and thereafter discarded. This was the main difference between the "tale proper" and the earlier magazine short prose narrative. The short prose narrative provided and continues to provide instant gratification and edification. The short story went beyond that to provide food for thought.

Wolfgang Hochbruck

Notes

[1] Washington Irving, *Tales of a Traveller, by Geoffrey Crayon, Gent.,* ed. Judith Giblin Haig (Boston: Twayne, 1987): 32.

² Fear of the French revolution proved the undoing of Thomas Paine, and both Irving and his contemporary James Fenimore Cooper were critical of European radicalism.

³ Göttingen, founded in 1732–34, was one of the most well-known German universities in the late 18th century. Many Americans studied in Göttingen because of its high reputation in philosophy, economics, and the liberal arts, including languages.

⁴ Immanuel Swedenborg was a Swedish philosopher and theologian (1688–1772) who emphasized the importance of empathy for the salvation of the individual. His later contention that he could speak to angels and spirits is suggested here as well.

⁵ The French revolution started in July 1789. The "reign of terror" which cost the lives of several thousand aristocrats, real as well as suspected counter-revolutionists, and eventually several of the most prominent heads of the revolutionary movement itself, did not come about until 1792–93. The statue of Henry IV, mentioned below, was overthrown in August 1792.

⁶ The Sorbonne, founded in 1268, is the oldest and most renowned of the universities of Paris.

⁷ Originally meaning "sandy bank," Place de Grève is the oldest part of Paris. The Hôtel de Ville (City Hall) mentioned here was destroyed during the Commune in 1871.

⁸ This deliberately ambiguous reading of the story follows Barbara Tepa Lupack, "Irving's German Student," *Studies in Short Fiction* 21.4 (1974): 398–400.

⁹ Simone Hagenmeyer, *Washington Irving und der periodical essay des 18. Jahrhunderts* (Göttingen: Cuvillier, 2000): 4.

¹⁰ Washington Irving, *Bracebridge Hall or The Humorists: A Medley by Geoffrey Crayon, Gent.*, ed. Herbert Smith (Washington: Twayne, 1977): 3.

¹¹ John Glendenning, "Irving and the Gothic Tradition," *Bucknell Review* 12.2 (1964): 91.

¹² Glendenning,"Irving and the Gothic Tradition" 97–98.

¹³ Lupack, "Irving's German Student" 399.

¹⁴ Lupack, "Irving's German Student" 399–400.

Magazine Sources

Anon. "Account of a Swiss Captain." *The American Museum* 1 (April, 1787).

____. "Adventure of a Young English Officer among the Abenakee Savages." *The Royal American Magazine* 2 (February, 1775).

Caloc. "Fidele: Or the Faithful Shepherd." *The Massachusetts Magazine* 3 (May, 1791).

Colla, Ruri. "The Story of the Captain's Wife and an Aged Woman." *Gentlemen and Ladies Town and Country Magazine* 1 (October/November, 1789).

Irving, Washington. "The Adventure of the German Student." *Tales of a Traveller. Part 1: Strange Stories by a Nervous Gentleman.* (1824).

Melpomene. "Yonora: An American Indian Tale." *The South Carolina Weekly Museum* 1 (January, 1797).

N. "Narrative of the Unpardonable Sin." *The Theological Magazine* 2 (1797).

Punctilio. "Story of Julia: A Real Character." *The Massachusetts Magazine* 2 (May/June, 1790).

Ramsay, James Rev. "The Desperate Negroe." *The Massachusetts Magazine* 10 (October, 1793).

Z. P. "Something Unaccountable." *The Massachusetts Magazine* 1 (September, 1789).

Further Reading

Short Story Collections

Current-Garcia, Eugene and Bert Hitchcock, eds. *American Short Stories*. New York: Longman, 1996.
Nagel, James, ed. *Anthology of the American Short Story*. Boston: Houghton Mifflin, 2007.
Pitcher, Edward W. R., ed. *An Anthology of the Short Story in 18th and 19th Century America*. 2 vols. Lewiston: Edwin Mellen P, 2000.

Historical Sources

Boorstin, Daniel J. *The Genius of American Politics*. Chicago: U of Chicago P, 1956.
Greene, Jack P. and J. R. Pole, eds. *A Companion to the American Revolution*. Malden, MA: Blackwell, 2000.
Hofstra, Warren R., ed. *Cultures in Conflict: The Seven Years' War in North America*. Lanham: Rowman, Littlefield, 2007.
Irving, Washington. *The Life and Letters of Washington Irving*. Ed. Pierre M. Irving. Vol. 2. New York: Putnam's, 1869. 3 vols.
Jefferson, Thomas. *Notes on the State of Virginia*. Ed. Thomas Perkins Abernethy. New York: Harper, Row, 1964.
Miller, Perry, ed. *The American Puritans: Their Prose and Poetry*. New York: Columbia UP, 1956.
Mott, Frank Luther. *A History of American Magazines: 1741-1850*. Cambridge, MA: Harvard UP, 1957.

Pitcher, Edward W. R. *Fiction in American Magazines before 1800*. Lewiston, N.Y.: Edwin Mellen P, 2002.
Riley, Sam G., ed. *American Magazine Journalists, 1741–1850*. Dictionary of Literary Biography 73. Detroit: Gales, 1988.

Critical Sources

Aarne, Antti and Stith Thompson. *The Types of the Folk Tales*. Helsinki: FF Communications, 1961.
Brown, Herbert Ross. *The Sentimental Novel in America 1789–1860*. New York: Pageant Books, 1956.
Carlson, C. Lennart. *The First Magazine: A History of the Gentleman's Magazine*. Providence: Brown UP, 1938.
Current-Garcia, Eugene. *The American Short Story before 1850: A Critical History*. Boston: Twayne, 1985.
Dittrich, Allan Bruce. *Characteristics of the Popular American Short Story, 1800–1850: An Anthology of Middle Class Fiction*. Diss. Brandeis U, 1977.
Gilmore, Michael T. "The Literature of the Revolutionary and Early National Periods."*The Cambridge History of American Literature. Vol. I: 1590–1820*. Gen. Ed. Sacvan Bercovitch. Cambridge: Cambridge UP, 1994: 539–693.
Görtschacher, Wolfgang and Holger Klein, eds. *Tale, Novella, Short Story: Currents in Short Fiction*. Tübingen: Stauffenburg Verlag, 2004.
Grey, James Louis. *The Development of the Early American Short Story to Washington Irving*. Diss. Duke U, 1971.
Hebel, Udo, ed. *The Construction and Contestation of American Culture and Identities in the Early National Period*. Heidelberg: C. Winter, 1999.
Koppelman, Susan. "A Preliminary Sketch of the Early History of U.S. Women's Short Stories." *Journal of American Culture* 22.2 (1999): 1–6.
Korte, Barbara. *The Short Story in Britain*. Tübingen: Francke UTB, 2003.

Lee, A. Robert and W. M. Verhoeven, eds. *Making America / Making American Literature: Franklin to Cooper*. Amsterdam: Rodopi, 1996.

Lloyd-Smith, Allan. *American Gothic Fiction*. New York: Continuum, 2004.

Lohafer, Susan and Jo Ellyn Clarey, eds. *Short Story Theory at a Crossroads*. Baton Rouge: Louisiana State UP, 1989.

Marler, Robert F. *The American Tale and Short Story*. Washington: UMI, 1979.

Matthews, Brander. *The Philosophy of the Short-Story in Pen and Ink*. New York: Longmans, Green, 1888.

Mogen, David, Scott P. Sanders, and Joanne B. Karpinski, eds. *Frontier Gothic: Terror and Wonder at the Frontier in American Literature*. Rutherford: Farleigh Dickinson UP, 1993.

Moore, Jack B. *Native Elements in American Magazine Short Fiction, 1741–1800*. Diss. U of North Carolina, 1963.

Pattee, Fred L. *The Development of the Short Story in America: An Historical Survey*. New York: Harper, 1923.

Poe, Edgar A. "Nathaniel Hawthorne: Twice-Told Tales." *The Complete Works of Edgar Allan Poe.* Ed. James A. Harrison. Vol. 11. New York: AMS P, 1965. 17 vols.

Strong, Pauline T. *Captive Selves, Captivating Others: The Politics and Poetics of Colonial American Captivity Narratives.* Boulder: Westview P, 1999.

Watson, Melvin R. *Magazine Serials and the Essay Tradition, 1746–1820*. Baton Rouge: Louisiana State UP, 1956.

www.ingramcontent.com/pod-product-compliance
Ingram Content Group UK Ltd.
Pitfield, Milton Keynes, MK11 3LW, UK
UKHW041945230426
12048UKWH00008B/146